M000222548

HOW TO WIN

"I am so happy to be married to Niki Winston! Niki is an amazing wife, and I'm glad that she is sharing with you the principles that she lives by. Any woman looking to get married, have a great marriage, or become a better woman should definitely read this book. I think this is RIGHT ON TARGET!"

- *David S. Winston, Pastor, Living Word Christian Center, Husband to Niki Winston*

"If you're looking for the latest "hook up" book, this isn't the one. With brilliant incision, Niki Winston cuts away all the myths of marriage and graciously gives you biblically based truth of what's really required to have a marriage that lasts a lifetime. A must read!"

- *Love McPherson, Relationship Expert and Author*

"Niki Winston is a leader, an extraordinary encourager and a powerful example of what a virtuous woman should be, reminding us every day, to love as He loves. How to Win Him and Keep Him Happy: Secrets to Becoming an Amazing Wife is an encouraging book filled with wisdom and godly advice not just for married women, but also for single women who are seeking "the one." Her unique ability to communicate in a profound yet practical way revolutionizes our understanding of marriage. Her heart is truly to see marriages become more powerful, enjoyable and easy. She reminds women that each season of life is special and part of a much bigger story in the plan of God!"

-   *Jacinth Katta, Founder, Ink Foundation, India*

"What makes this read so powerful is the life of the author. Niki's transparency, honesty and wisdom on each page position this book as "the gospel of relationships" according to proof positive theology. My wife and I knowing Niki and her husband intimately for years adds more value to the idea that the pages are not just theories but a lifestyle of fruitfulness that has deeply impacted our very own marriage. Anyone looking for love in or out of marriage you've found yourself with the right tool in this book."

-   *Calvin & English Battle, Pastors, Destiny Center, Tulsa*

HOW TO WIN HIM

AND KEEP

HIM HAPPY

Secrets to Becoming an AMAZING Wife

NIKIWINSTON

ISBN 978-0-9976944-3-7
Published by Better Life Group

Design by: Jabez Design & Marketing
www.jabezdesignmarketing.com

www.nikiwinston.org

To my AMAZING husband, David,
who is literally and without exaggeration, the most
incredible, supportive husband on
the face of planet Earth.
I pray you reap on the countless seeds
that you have sown in my life.
I love you more.

Contents

INTRODUCTION | Preparation Precedes Success   1

SECTION 1
How to Keep Him Happy

CHAPTER ONE | Marriage Done Right   7

CHAPTER TWO | Let it Go and Keep it Moving: The Importance of Forgiveness   31

CHAPTER THREE | Your Self-Esteem's Profound Effect on Your Marriage   47

CHAPTER FOUR | Don't Be Eve   63

CHAPTER FIVE | Letting Him Off the Hook   79

CHAPTER SIX | Men Are Simple: A Man's Three Basic Needs   97

SECTION 2
How to Win Him

CHAPTER SEVEN | Being "Attractive"   129

He who finds a wife finds a good thing,

And obtains favor from the Lord.

Proverbs 18:22, NKJV

INTRODUCTION

Preparation Precedes Success

God has a plan for your life. It is undoubtedly, decidedly so. Not for one second do I hesitate to say to you that there is an important and very specific purpose for your life, and it quite possibly involves a man. Yes, I'm referring to your (future) husband. When you marry, not only is it one of the single most important decisions you can ever make, it also becomes part of your God-given destiny. You must take it very seriously. This person becomes deeply intertwined with whatever it is that you're supposed to do while here on this Earth. Don't be caught off-guard. Be prepared. Be ready for what is to come. I not only recommend reading *this* book, but also reading a number of others (resources listed in the back of the book), going to pre-marital classes, watching online videos, and even taking college courses if they'll help! Do whatever you can to prepare for marriage, and if you're already married, get better at it! We should never stop growing, always continuing to press toward maturity and perfection.

Secondly, let's get one thing straight: This book is written with the assumption that your husband (or future husband) is a good, God-fearing man who loves you properly, and has the best intentions for you and your marriage. It is always implied, when I'm speaking to Christian women, that the man they will end up with will also be Christian. I don't generally feel the need to address this issue because it is non-negotiable; a deal-breaker, as many say. So if you notice that I don't talk about him being a Christian man when referring to your husband or future husband, it is because I assume that if you are smart enough to buy this book, you are smart enough to know that a strong Christian and a non-Christian don't mix well in marriage (2 Cor. 6:14). If you are a Christian woman already married to a non-Christian, don't be discouraged. The Word of God has something for you. You WILL win him to Christ! (1 Pet. 3:1)

And lastly, I want to say this to the single ladies: because I believe in dinner before dessert, preparation before enjoyment and responsibilities before fun, I have saved the "fun" stuff until the end. The book may be called How to Win Him and Keep Him Happy, but chronologically, you will read how to "keep him happy" (and essentially how to be an amazing wife) before you read the section on "winning him." We should all be doing things decently and in order (1 Cor. 14:40), and we don't really have any business "winning" a man if we don't know how to "keep him happy," now do we?

Enjoy!

SECTION 1

HOW TO KEEP HIM HAPPY

Chapter 1
Marriage Done Right

We all have this fantasy of the perfect, most amazing man: a relentless provider with a chiseled jaw, even more chiseled abs and big strong hands that long to hold us tightly every night. It's with those same hands that he reaches out to grasp ours every single morning, leading us in prayer. He loves us unconditionally, and we know this because he never criticizes us and never ceases to tell us how amazing we are multiple times per day. In his eyes, we are the picture of perfection, unable to do any wrong. He loves every bump, lump and wrinkle on us, and wouldn't change a thing about our personality, habits, body or behavior.

We all want to be loved unconditionally and intensely, but even though you absolutely deserve it, that's not what marriage is about. If I ask why you want to be married and the answer is that you want someone to love

7

you, as pure-hearted as it may sound, you're headed in the wrong direction. We must completely change our attitude about marriage. We've got to move out of a receiving posture and into a giving position. Marriage should not be about what a man can give you, whether it be a sense of love, affirmation and approval, provision, stability, status, sex, or even a feeling of completion. We can't go into a relationship, looking primarily to get our needs met. This is a narcissistic attitude, and no man is on his knees anywhere, asking God to send him a needy, selfish woman. Marriage is not about who can love you, take care of you, fill all your emotional "holes" and make it so that you don't have to work anymore. It's about who YOU can love, serve, and take care of. Marriage takes a selfless, servanthood attitude from BOTH parties. It's work, yes, but it's absolutely worth it. If you come into relationships and marriage with the attitude of "How much can I add to this person's life", I guarantee it will make you HAPPY.

Think of it: you get the PRIVILEGE of connecting with another human spirit to become a more powerful force for the purpose that God, the creator of the universe, has planted inside of you. Today I am challenging you to pull up your boot straps and be a full-grown woman. Change your entire perspective on how you see marriage. Instead of saying cliché things like, "I want to share my life with someone," say "I want to serve like there is no tomorrow." Instead of just wanting someone to love you, foster a desire to add to someone's life so that they can fulfill their God-given purpose. Develop a desire to link up with someone to produce fruit and to make a difference in your home, your family, your community and your WORLD.

> *We must completely change our attitude about marriage. We've got to move out of a receiving posture, and into a giving position.*

In this first chapter, we will cultivate a proper attitude toward marriage by exploring three areas: learning selflessness, developing a heart for serving others and understanding the true purpose of marriage.

LEARN SELFLESSNESS

Selfishness is the number one cause of divorce and unhappy marriages. No matter what the obvious issue is that you are facing in your marriage, if you're selfish, you will fail. You may be able to stay married, but if you stay selfish, you're doing it wrong. However, if you and your spouse can learn to be selfless, then I believe you can survive anything. No one is naturally fully selfless. True selflessness must be learned and developed. By "fully" I do not mean 100% selfless, without any room to fall short. If we were required to be perfectly selfless, exactly like Jesus, in order to stay happily married, then all of us would be miserable and divorced.

Don't misunderstand me. In Philippians 3:12 we are asked to press toward perfection. Perfecting our Christ-like attributes should always be the goal, striving to get better and more perfect in the love of Christ, no matter how far along we think we are. And the word "press" implies that we will encounter resistance. We must actually put in WORK to become more selfless - more like Jesus. It's with effort, time, and persistence in this 'pressing' that we begin to see the perfection that Paul talks about in Philippians.

Jesus is by far the best example of selflessness we've ever seen. He was selfless to a degree that many of us would find extremely uncomfortable, even impossible. Let's take a look in Matthew 14 at the high standard of selflessness that He has set for us in the Bible. This passage begins as King Herod has just had John, Jesus' cousin beheaded in prison:

So he sent and had John beheaded in prison. And his head was brought on a platter and given to the girl, and she brought it to her mother. Then his disciples came and took away the body and buried it, and went and told Jesus. When Jesus heard it, He departed from there by boat to a deserted place by Himself. But when the multitudes heard it, they followed Him on foot from the cities. And when Jesus went out He saw a great multitude; and He was moved with compassion for them, and healed their sick. (Matt. 14:10-14, NKJV)

When I really took note of what was happening here, I was in awe. Probably one of the most important people on Earth to Jesus, John was not only a close family member, and arguably his most faithful follower, but he was also THE ONE who proclaimed Jesus to all and led people into Christ's repentance and baptism.

John, a man whom Jesus loved dearly, had just gotten beheaded, a despicable and undignified death. It clearly states that Jesus went to a deserted place to be by Himself. It can be assumed that Jesus went to grieve. He probably wanted to sort through His feelings, talk to God about it, pray, cry, and give His emotions a chance to "run their course," so He could move on properly. But when the multitudes heard He went away, they followed Him. Now as we ponder this scripture, we see a hurting man with valid feelings, just wanting a little time to Himself, and rightfully so. We also see a selfish and inconsiderate group of people, following Him to pull on His gifts and take from Him whatever it is that they feel that they "need." It can also be assumed that these people knew that His cousin had died, and it says that they heard that He had gone off to be by Himself. So they

12

KNEW He wanted alone time and still bombarded Him! Instead of Jesus doing what was expected: justifiably making them wait and insisting on His time alone, what does the Bible say He did? He had compassion for THEM. When it was HE who was hurting the most, He healed their sick.

Selflessness is powerful. Selflessness doesn't insist on its own rights. No. Instead, selflessness has compassion for those around it, even in the midst of the worst circumstances. It is a powerful, healing force to everyone around. If you can be truly selfless, you can be the change agent in your family, helping to heal all of those in your circle of influence. You can stay in the will of God, walking in love, no matter how difficult the situations are with which you are faced.

LIVE SELFLESSLY AS A LIFESTYLE

If we want to be happy in marriage, we must learn to live a lifestyle of selflessness. Being selfless encompasses many things, so in an effort to make learning selflessness easier, we are going to take a look at its arch enemy: selfishness.

13

No marriage can survive two selfish spouses. Selfishness is "I" focused. It is defensive and demanding. It wants what it wants and "needs" it immediately. It's a lying hypocrite, doing whatever seems best for itself at the moment, and not considering those around it. Selfishness is lazy and it doesn't like to work, especially for the benefit of others. It's jealous, interprets other people's communication negatively, and is full of pride. If you start asking a selfish person questions about themselves, chances are they will start to become defensive, and eventually end up offended, even if they are innocent, open-ended questions. You may say, "What did you do today?" However, they hear "What did you do all day? Don't you

> *Selfishness assumes the worst and is quick to speak. No marriage can survive two selfish spouses.*

have anything to show for yourself?" Or, they may hear, "I know you've been doing something that I disapprove of... Just admit to it so I can judge you." Selfishness assumes the worst. Selfishness is a victim.

Selfishness is also quick to speak. When the selfish spouse hears a question like the aforementioned one,

14

they don't take a moment to say to themselves, "Maybe my negative interpretation is incorrect. I shouldn't assume the worst. Why don't I just answer their question without any pretense?" Instead, selfishness hears the question, filters it through their negative, self-focused filter, and spews out the first defensive, prideful thing that comes to mind. Proverbs 29:11 says that a fool vents all his feelings. Selfishness is foolish, and it keeps you in bondage. It knows no peace, like a terrible disease of the soul. Unless you learn the opposite of selfishness, your soul only gets sicker and sicker, eventually creating physical manifestations of this sickness (Prov. 14:30).

SELFLESSNESS

Selflessness is exactly the opposite. Selflessness is so freeing and peaceful! Imagine right now a wife who is selfish. Now imagine her levels of peace and her levels of misery. Now imagine a wife who is selfless. She loves to give, and thinks not of herself, but of others first. What do you think her soul looks like? Is it full of peace and rest? Yes. She's joyful and confident, knowing that the hearts of people around her are safe. When you are at peace, you can be a healing agent for those around you, as opposed to a toxin. It is a very fulfilling and peaceful place to be, when you are selfless.

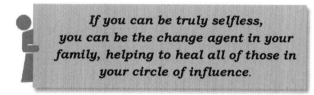

If you can be truly selfless, you can be the change agent in your family, helping to heal all of those in your circle of influence.

So what is selflessness? In a word, it's CONSIDERATION. When you are selfless, you are constantly considering others. You are not asking what it is YOU need at the moment. Conversely, you are asking what the others around you might need. In marriage, a situation might look like this:

Joe came home late that evening from a particularly difficult day of work. He had made all of his usual shipments, which normally takes about nine hours, including loading and unloading all of the merchandise on and off the truck. Today however, because of someone else's clerical mistake, all of the slips were missing in each of the deliveries. At the end of the

16

day he normally brings his truck back in, clocks out, and heads home. But as he was pulling in, one of the retailers called the office and told them what they had discovered. Because of this mistake, Joe had to drive his entire route of over 100 miles over again and drop off slips to all the same places that he had already driven to earlier that day. To top it off, the extra time didn't add to his paycheck proportionately, because Joe gets the majority of his pay on commissions, and he was not receiving any commission for this extra work he was doing. Joe arrived home over three hours late, dirty, tired, and extremely hungry, not to mention upset and frustrated about this unavoidable problem that he had to face today.

Elaine had also experienced a particularly difficult day. Home all day with three young children, there are already many challenges one can encounter, but today was a bit harder. Because of things that came up with the new baby, she got out to do the weekly grocery shopping later than usual. Because of this,

17

she ended up at the grocery store during the naptime of the two eldest, who are three and five years old, and if this weren't already a challenge, the baby needed to nurse while they were there. So there is Elaine, stuck on a bench, nursing a baby with two tired children, one fussing, the other crying, and all she wanted was to get some groceries to feed her family. When she got home, she still needed to put the groceries away, but found that water had leaked all over the kitchen floor because the dishwasher was not closed properly. Then, after making dinner, Elaine got a short call from her agitated husband saying that he would not be home to keep the children during her exercise class because he had to stay hours late to fix a mistake that someone else made. Elaine's exercise class was the one thing that she does by herself, for herself since the new baby was born, and boy did she ever need it that day, but it just wasn't happening. Let's just say it was a trying day for both.

So there they were: 8:30pm, Elaine had already fed the kids, ALONE, and Joe is getting home just as she has finished putting the last child to bed, ALONE. Elaine is DONE and can't help but feel a little frustrated; like she could use some comforting. As soon as she sees Joe, she says, "Oh thank God you're here. I had the hardest day. I could really use a hug." Joe quickly retorts, "Well, you're not the only one who had a hard day. I need a shower and a meal. Then you can talk to me about your problems."

> **Consideration:**
> **When you are selfless, you are constantly considering others.**

Joe quickly storms off toward the nearest bathroom – no hug, no kiss. Joe was obviously being short and insensitive, and it made Elaine feel worse than before. Elaine has a choice here: Does she consider herself and her feelings? Or does she do the selfless thing and figure out what her husband needs?

Let's take a lesson in selflessness: Elaine has a right to be loved. She has a right to receive a hug from her husband after a long frustrating day. Her feelings of discontentment and her desire to be comforted by her husband are valid and justified. Selfishness would demand those things from him. Selflessness, however, is truly considerate. Elaine has a decision to make: should she get upset at her husband's insensitivity and demand a hug or a listening ear? Or should she decide to be considerate and understanding - discerning what it is that he might need and try her best to give it to him - not expecting anything in return?

Do you remember Jesus, after his friend was murdered, and He went away to be alone and grieve? He deserved that time, but He GAVE. He considered the problems of the people, even the ones whose problems were smaller than His. Even the ones who were being insensitive and inconsiderate, and He gave them everything He had, while expecting nothing in return. If we can take this approach in marriage, oh what a happier place this world (and your home) will be! Jesus' selflessness should inspire us to give to those that which they do not deserve, and then expect nothing back from them in return.

Elaine could have decided to give Joe a little space, and then come back again later for her hug and comfort, taking a little something from Joe that she felt he had to give. But what if she did just that and then later, he still wasn't feeling better and disappointed her again? Then she would have felt that her efforts to "make peace" were in vain because they did not get her what she wanted in the first place. This is why it is so important NOT to expect anything in return. The disappointment from not receiving what you expected (and it will come) can make the matter even worse, putting more tension on the marriage relationship. **True selflessness relinquishes any expectation of recompense on a good act.** If Elaine decided to "let Joe off the hook," and give him his space, she should not expect to be "paid back" with a kind act from Joe later.

Albeit difficult, mustering possibly the last stitch of patience and self-control that she has in her that day, the best choice from Elaine would have been to read her

husband, using what she knows about him, his temper-
ament, and how he usually handles frustration, and do
her best to give him what he may need. THIS IS AN ACT
OF LOVE. **Love gives others what they do not deserve.** She could have taken a breath, smiled (if possible)
and said, "Yes dear, you must be so hungry after working
so hard all day. You go get your shower and I'll heat your
dinner for you. Is there anything else you need from me
right now?" The amount of love and respect emanating
from that response could have been enough to turn her
husband's whole day around, and doing this with no
ulterior motive is truly selfless. *Her joy can be found that
day in bringing peace to her husband.*

> *Jesus' selflessness should inspire us
> to give to those that which they do
> not deserve and then expect nothing
> back from them in return.*

Selflessness sounds exhausting, but it's not; it's life-
giving to you, and to your relationships. It is an attitude
that causes you to reap peace in your heart and in your
relationships. A person doesn't become selfless overnight. It takes forethought, deliberate strategizing and

self-training. It is effort, but over time, and with practice, being selfless becomes more and more effortless. Don't focus on not being selfish. Strive to become selfless and selfishness will soon fade away. Lastly, remember that selflessness, just like all principles that come from the Word of God, is a seed. When you plant a seed, you do not see a tree right away; but if you don't lose heart, you will reap in due season (Gal. 6:9).

Meditate on this:

Love suffers long and is kind (endures with patience and serenity, and is kind and thoughtful); love is not jealous; love does not brag nor is it proud or arrogant. It is not rude; it is not self-seeking. Love is not overly sensitive and easily angered. It thinks no evil; It does not rejoice at iniquity (the consequences of sin), but rejoices when right and truth prevail. Love always protects, always trusts, believing the best in each one, always hopes, remaining steadfast during difficult times, and always perseveres and endures without weakening. Love never fails. (Paraphrased, 1Cor. 13:4-8 AMP, NKJV, NIV)

23

AN ATTITUDE OF SERVITUDE

Sometimes it's not as easy as Joe and Elaine's situation. Theirs is actually a very simple example of selflessness, but often times we find ourselves in a relationship where we think we are giving all we know to give

> *Don't focus on not being selfish. Strive to become selfless and selfishness will soon fade away.*

and not seeming to affect our spouse as we had hoped. You must ask yourself, "What is my motive in my giving?" Are you serving in order to receive? Are you trying to get a reaction or a specific response? *Love is free.* If you are giving to your spouse, check your motives. The best kind of service is service without expectation of recompense. Are you giving freely, or giving to get something? A selfless person is constantly checking their motives. This is extremely important and something you should do as a lifestyle. Daily, I recommend you say this quick prayer I found in Psalms. This will keep your motives pure in all things, including serving your spouse.

Search me [thoroughly], O God, and know my heart; Test me and know my anxious thoughts; And see if there is any wicked or hurtful way in me, And lead me in the everlasting way. (Ps. 139:23-24, AMP)

Serving others is not just a thing that someone does. It is not just an act or a verb; it is a heart. We must *develop* a heart to serve others. This heart of service, just like selflessness, does not usually come naturally. It must be learned, trained and developed. We can learn service from Jesus. Jesus was the greatest example of servanthood ever to live on the Earth. Everything He did was for others. He almost never did anything for Himself. When He wasn't specifically serving other people around Him, He was asking God, the Father, what He wanted for Him to do or say next. Every Word that came out of Jesus' mouth was for others; everywhere He went, He went for others, and everything He did, He did for others.

Jesus said,

> *Very truly I tell you, whoever believes in me will do the works I have been doing, and they will do even greater things than these, because I am going to the Father. And I will do whatever you ask in my name, so that the Father may be glorified in the Son. You may ask me for anything in my name, and I will do it.* (Jn. 14:12-14, NKJV)

This tells us two things: First, we can serve like Jesus did. He says that if we believe in Him, we can do even greater things than what He did while He was on the Earth! We have the capacity in us to serve even greater than Jesus did while He was on Earth. We must own that truth and embrace it. Secondly, we can ask God for a heart to serve, and Jesus will give it to us. Jesus Himself said that we may ask Him for ANYTHING in His name and He will do it. Is a love for service "anything?" Then if we just ask, He will give it to us. You can say this prayer out loud, right now:

Jesus, You said that if I ask You for anything, in Your name, that You will do it. I know that You want me to have a heart to serve others as You did, so I ask that, right now, You give me a heart to serve like You, with no selfish motives. Develop in me a love for serving others. I ask in Your name, so that the Father may be glorified in the Son. Help me to show Your love through Christ-like service. In the name of Jesus Christ of Nazareth, Amen.

THE PURPOSE OF MARRIAGE

I mentioned at the beginning of this chapter that you get the privilege of connecting with another human spirit to be a more powerful force for the purpose that God has planted inside of you. The purpose of marriage is powerful. In chapter two, you will learn more about the concept that God works in multiplication; but let's take a quick look at Deuteronomy 32:30. It starts off by saying *"How could one chase a thousand, And two put ten thousand to flight..."* (NKJV). Immediately, two things stand out in this scripture. First, when there is one person, they have the capacity to only chase their adversaries, painting the picture of ground combat. A different picture is painted when there are two standing together and the enemy is put to *flight*. The other thing we see here are the numbers: With God, one can stand against a thousand, but two people can stand *together* against ten thousand. What we can conclude from this small portion of scripture is that we are ten times

> *We have the capacity in us to serve even greater than Jesus did while He was on Earth.*

more powerful when we are two, together, and our supernatural power and abilities are greatly magnified as well (causing our enemies to fly away, as opposed to the necessity of ground pursuit). If we are so much more powerful together, and we know that God has called each one of us to a purpose, then why wouldn't our purpose be exponentially greater *together*?

I remember when my husband and I first got together. It was as if we were both on our own path in life, but when we connected, we made this powerful B-line toward God and His plan for our lives. It was clear that we were the right choice for each other because our being together caused both of us to chase after God as individuals more than ever before. We knew that our destinies were powerfully tied together. **The right person will cause you to run toward God, not hide from Him.**

If our primary purpose in marriage is to be a more powerful force for the Kingdom of God, and we can keep this at the forefront of our focus, then it is difficult to become selfish. How can I be focused on my feelings and what I think I'm lacking, or injustices I feel that are being done to me, if I am consumed with a desire to serve God and His people with my marriage? God can only get things done in this Earth through His people. He needs YOU to be ready and available, through the powerful force of your marital union, to do His work, to serve His creation. This should motivate you to stay in unity within your marriage. Do it unto God. Do it as a service. Do it selflessly.

I would like to end this section on *The Purpose of Marriage* with a quote that I love from my husband, as he was teaching on destiny and relationships.

"If I ever walked away from my wife, then I would be walking away from God, because I KNOW that she is a major part of my God-given destiny."

-Pastor David S. Winston

Chapter 2

Let it Go and Keep It Moving

The Importance of Forgiveness

In this chapter, I really want to capture God's heart for forgiveness. When God sent Jesus, He was sending the message that, "Even though you've disobeyed Me, betrayed Me, blasphemed My name, and have completely rejected My love and all of My provision, I am willing to make the greatest sacrifice that a man can make, JUST to forgive you – to let you off the hook." **Forgiveness is a sacrifice. It is difficult, and it takes great strength, effort, love and FAITH.** The Bible says, *"Whenever you stand praying, if you have anything against anyone, forgive him [drop the issue, let it go], so that your Father who is in heaven will also forgive you* *your transgressions and wrongdoings [against Him and others]"* (Mark 11:25, AMP). We know that forgiveness is an act of love, and therefore if we are not forgiving, we are not walking fully in love. The Bible also says that our faith works by love (Gal. 5:6, KJV), so we can conclude that if we are not walking in love by forgiving others, our faith is rendered ineffective. If our faith is not effective, and we are asking God to forgive our sins, BY FAITH, how then can He forgive us? Anything you are trying to do by faith WILL NOT WORK if you have unforgiveness in your heart - including prayer for your marriage. Even prayer for you to improve and be a blessing as a wife, and for your husband to operate in wisdom and love you properly can be hindered when there is bitterness in your heart. This is a powerful and profound revelation, if you catch it.

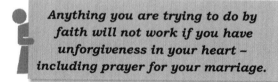

Anything you are trying to do by faith will not work if you have unforgiveness in your heart – including prayer for your marriage.

Not only does unforgiveness hinder your faith and, therefore, EVERY SINGLE ONE of your prayers, but it hinders your heart as well. Forgiveness is the first step in being whole, and without wholeness, your marriage could be doomed. Let me explain:

In chapter one we touched on the fact that God works in multiplication. The Bible tells us that one (person) can chase a thousand, but two can put TEN thousand to FLIGHT (Deut. 32:30). We know that this means that the power that is in us is exponentially *multiplied* when we team up with someone! The Bible also says that when a man and a woman marry, that the TWO of them become ONE (Eph. 5:31). Well, anyone who's taken second grade math knows that 1x1=1. If God was a God of addition, then He would say that when a man and woman come together, they become TWO; but instead, God decided to *multiply*. Even the laws of sowing and reaping show that God MULTIPLIES. By now, I assume you're asking, "Ok Niki, what does this have to do with how I can 'win' a man and keep him happy?" Well, this is a bit of a deep point I'm making, so stay with me...

Wholeness is essential to a healthy marriage. If God multiplies: If 1x1=1, then it is extremely important that we enter a marriage WHOLE. Throughout life, we are often a victim of circumstances. Parents fall short or even get divorced; people may have done you physical or psychological harm, abused, molested, or even raped you. Outside forces could have left you feeling alone, abandoned, neglected, even homeless and more. There are so many wounds and pains you could have fallen victim to in your life, in childhood or adulthood. There are even the self-inflicted pains of bad decisions. There is no doubt that these things can leave us broken in pieces. We would absolutely be lying to ourselves if we were to say that we were not affected by the sins of our past (Remember: You can be hurt by both sins committed AGAINST you and sins committed BY you). When you are broken, it is safe to say you are not whole. This is exactly what the word "broken" means. You are a piece or a part: a fraction of the whole person that God wants you to be. So for the sake of this example, let's say you're a half. Oftentimes, because of the laws of attraction, a half of a person attracts a half of a person: two broken people who have not fully dealt with all of the pain of their past. Well, if God works in multiplication, which He

34

does, then what do we get when we multiply a half of a person with a half? That's right: $\frac{1}{2} \times \frac{1}{2} = \frac{1}{4}$. A quarter! How is this possible, you ask?

When you're whole, you can deal with difficult situations in a healthy way. Problems will undoubtedly arise in your marriage. It is not confessing something negative over your marriage to say so. The Bible even says that we will fall into many different types of trials (problems), but in the end of that same verse, we are told that we should be perfect and entire (whole) (James 1:2-4). What happens when two broken people find each other is this: When they encounter these inevitable "trials" (money problems, jealousy, mistreatment, problems with in-laws, career changes and overall discontentment, just to name a few), instead of being able to address these issues from a whole, healthy place, they often come from a place of hurt, shame or fear. When your husband does something hurtful or offensive to you, do you know it is your job to cover his offense with love? (Prov. 10:12) This is what a whole person does. They don't retaliate, they don't reject, they don't "teach them a lesson" and they definitely don't give them a piece of their mind. If this sounds hard, that's because it is. That's why it is important to pursue wholeness BEFORE getting married. When a couple is comprised of two "halves," so to speak, they respond *to* offense *with* offense. They tear each other down. They stay in defense mode and hurt each other continually until there is but a remnant left of the person that they married. A half-husband can easily tear a half-wife into a quarter and vice versa. This is how the enemy can take God's holy and powerful law of multiplication and use it for evil.

Forgiveness is the key to getting whole. Before you should pursue any lifelong commitment to another living being, do both of yourselves a favor and start down the path of forgiveness. Wholeness is a 3-step process: FORGIVENESS, HEALING and HABIT CHANGES. But forgiveness MUST come first! (For more information on this, see my book *How to Be Whole*, 2017.) Let's make sure to get one thing straight: When you forgive someone, it is for YOU (the "victim"), not for THEM (the trespasser).

Forgiveness releases the hold that someone else has on your life. Most times, when you forgive someone, it has no effect on the other person. It is for you only. I will use an example of something I see far too often: If you were molested by a friend of your parent as a child, chances are you have never forgotten about it. Let's

> *Forgiveness releases the hold that someone else has on your life.*

say, in this situation, the other person has moved on with their life. They have a family, a career, and are living on the other side of the country. In that moment that you face the decision to forgive them, you are aware that they don't deserve your forgiveness. It can feel like if you do forgive them, that somehow you're doing something nice or good for them, but you're not.

When I am working with ladies who have been through something like this, and am walking them through a forgiveness proxy, especially when they are having a tough time letting the person who violated them "off the hook," I tell them this: "At the moment that you forgive them, they will feel nothing. They will be completely unaffected, having no idea of what you just did.

If they are happy right now, they will stay happy, and if they are miserable at this moment, they will stay miserable. The only one who will feel anything right now is you. And what you will feel is freedom." When you forgive someone, you are saying, *I will no longer be defined by what you did to me. I'm no longer going to be affected, angry or bitter about something that I couldn't control. What I CAN control now is my reaction, and I've decided to disconnect from you and release the hold that you have on me and my emotions.*

When you do this, you feel a brand new freedom, like you've never felt before, and you are full speed ahead on the road to becoming a whole person.

HOW TO FORGIVE

Sometimes it's easier said than done to forgive, and sometimes we don't forgive, simply because we really don't know where to start. There are many ways that you can approach forgiveness, but today we will go over **Three Forgiveness Techniques.**

1. Forgiveness Proxy (with a partner)

I believe a forgiveness proxy is probably the most effective way to approach initial forgiveness, especially if you are forgiving someone for what you feel like is a major event in your life (e.g., abuse, abandonment or neglect, sexual assault, rejection, issues related to a divorce, custody, cheating, stealing, etc.) because it addresses the person head-on without them having to be present.

In a forgiveness proxy you need a partner. The partner will stand-in for the transgressor. You would start out by letting your partner know the name of your transgressor (if possible) and what they did to you. In this situation we will use a father who abandoned his daughter, named Sheila. The script might go something like this:

(While standing face to face...)

Transgressor: *Sheila, I am your dad (or insert name here). I am so sorry for leaving you. I am so glad that you have come to forgive me because there is no excuse for what I've done, and it wasn't your fault. You deserved to have me in your life and I wasn't there. I was wrong and I hurt you. Do you forgive me?*

Sheila: *Yes, I forgive you, dad... And I release you.*

Transgressor: *Thank you so much for forgiving me. I love you. You're a good daughter.*

(Sheila and Transgressor hug.)

It is important to make sure to include a few things in a forgiveness proxy:

- Call the transgressor by name.
- The transgressor should state what they did wrong and apologize.
- The forgiver must tell the transgressor that they forgive them (by name). They can also say that they release them, if the situation warrants this.
- The transgressor should respond to the forgiveness, gratefully, and I personally think it helps with the healing process to add something that you feel the Lord would want them to know (i.e., *"I love you.*

You're a good daughter."). Be led as to what to say. God will lead you.

2. Forgive on paper

Another technique, which I like, is writing everyone down that you can think of that you have any ought against. If you think of the person, and a bad feeling comes, write them down. This list can be simple and direct. You can only mention names, or you can write down every single thing that you can think of. If these details matter to you, don't miss anything. Take a few days and make sure you write all of the wrongdoings and trespasses that these people are guilty of in your eyes. Even if you're not absolutely sure they were wrong, write it down.

After your list is complete, you can pray, OUT LOUD and privately. Keep the list before your eyes, mentioning all of the names of the people that you're forgiving, as well as verbalizing the fact that you forgive them. I don't think it's a great idea to verbalize what they did. Writing it down is enough, and you no longer need to rehearse the wrong that they've done. Rehearsing a negative memory can deepen its roots and, in turn, their effects: *the tree and its fruit* (For more information on this, also see my book *How to Be Whole*, 2017.) Once you are done with the prayer, DO NOT KEEP IT. You can light the paper on fire (but be safe), rip it up and throw it away or run over it with your car. I don't care what you do to it, but make sure to symbolically destroy and discard it because it is no longer yours.

3. Forgive to yourself

This is simply calling out the person by name (out loud – this is important) and telling them you forgive them. Obviously, it is important to go where others can't hear you, and to prepare your heart, making sure you mean it. You can do this as many times as you need to, for as many people as is needed. I really only recommend this as a last resort, or for only minor offenses that don't seriously affect the course of your life. Although this option is effective, the first two options may be even more fruitful, at least initially, until you have really built up your faith for forgiveness. Once you're an old pro, this technique can come in handy and work just as well as the others (For more information on this, see my book *How to Forgive Everyone*, 2017.)

STAYING IN FORGIVENESS

Imagine a pocket. Not the jeans kind. Imagine one shaped like one of those velvet bags with the drawstring, except this one is see-through. Now imagine it's inside of you – somewhere near your belly where you picture your spirit to be. This is your forgiveness faith-pocket. It's where you keep your faith for forgiveness. Right now, it may be full of the wrong things, like fear, anger,

> *If your man of God is not obeying the Word, it is implied that you will need to be walking in forgiveness with him.*

bitterness, resentment, and anxiety, but hopefully not. If forgiveness is an area where you have already gained understanding and have exercised your faith, then it is likely your forgiveness faith-pocket is nice and full! Congratulations! For those of us who are newer to the idea of actively forgiving - or forgiving "by faith" - our pockets may need some reworking.

Romans 10:17 says that faith comes by hearing the Word of God. The key words here are *faith, hearing* and *Word of God.* If we want *faith*, it only comes through actual *hearing* – through our ears – from words spoken out loud. Which kind of words though? It is The *Word of God.* When we forgive someone, the enemy will often try to come almost immediately to convince us that it didn't work. He wants us to believe that we didn't forgive, and we still have the exact same feelings toward that person as before. This is a lie! We must know how to combat the fiery darts of the wicked one. It's with the Word of God! So when you forgive someone and those bad feelings try to rise up, we speak the Word over ourselves, out loud, to build our faith. You say, "Oh no! I forgave that person! The Word says that I can forgive 70 x 7 to just one person alone (Matt. 18:21-22)! That's 490 times, and even for doing the same thing, over and over! I forgive them, Lord! In Jesus' name, and by the power of the Holy Spirit, they are FORGIVEN!" You may have to do this often, but in doing it you are filling up that forgiveness faith-pocket and before you know it, your faith to forgive will be strong, and exercising it will come easily!

Lastly, I encourage you to *stay* in faith for forgiveness. Not only will you need it to become a whole and free person, making you a better wife, but I can guarantee you that your wonderful and loving husband will give you opportunity to flex your forgiveness muscles on a regular basis. We are all human, and we all say or do offensive things at times. In 1Peter 3:1, it talks about the husband who does not obey the Word. God does not instruct the wife to leave this man. He essentially tells her to win him back by her humility, honoring him and being submissive. If you've married a man, I'm going to assume that you were under the impression that he was a man of God. If your man of God is not obeying the Word, it is implied that you will need to be walking in forgiveness with him, true forgiveness, that is powered by love, which covers a multitude of sins (Proverbs 10:12). If you are truly *covering* his sins and his faults, then you will still respect and honor that man as if he had never sinned. This is the forgiveness that you will need to be walking in: Powerful "forgiveness-faith."

Chapter 3
Your Self-Esteem's Profound Effect on Your Marriage

Your self-esteem has a profoundly powerful effect on your marriage. To properly address this issue, let me first talk about the meaning that we are assigning to the term "self-esteem" in this chapter. Self-esteem can be defined many ways, but I am referring to the view you have of yourself. **If you have a twisted, incorrect, negative, or conversely, an elevated view of yourself, you can sabotage your conversations, interactions, arguments, and eventually your relationships.**

Low self-esteem can cause to you to make bad decisions, be defensive, say spiteful and hurtful things, and it can cause your mood to rise and fall at your husband's word. Once you're married, to you he is the most important human person on this Earth. Of course his opinions will matter most to you. They should. But when you see yourself in the proper light (proper self-esteem), you are not defined by your husband's opinions.

RIGHTEOUSNESS: THE KEY TO YOUR SELF-ESTEEM

Proper self-esteem allows you to be your best you, but how can you be your best you unless you know who that is? Let's take Matthew 5:44 for example. It tells us to love our enemies and pray for those who persecute us. Now imagine someone in your lifetime that you have considered your enemy. Have you ever had someone persecute you? Who was it? Was your initial response with that person to love and pray for them? Now, let's be clear that praying in this example is not referring to praying for their safety from you causing them harm. "Lord, keep me Christian. Help me not to haul off and punch them in the throat." It's also not referring to you praying for them to be fixed, or even worse, punished. "Lord, you said vengeance is Yours, so go get 'em! Let them fall and hurt their leg because Your Word says pride comes before the fall... Father, let their limp be a humbling reminder to them of the error of their ways."

You wouldn't pray for their destruction. That's called witchcraft. Prayer with ulterior motives is manipulation, and righteousness doesn't manipulate. Instead, you would pray for them the same way you would pray for your child or a loving friend. You would do it in love, with the best motives, wanting to bless their life.

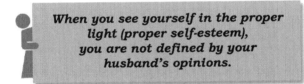

> When you see yourself in the proper light (proper self-esteem), you are not defined by your husband's opinions.

This is what the best you looks like. It is someone who can walk in love at all times. We are all a work in progress, but the end goal that we should all be working toward is *perfect love*. Perfect love never gets offended. Do you want that? Do you want the ability to walk around, not concerned with what anyone thinks of you, but God? Do you want to never be hurt because someone important to you criticized you harshly, or worse, completely ignored you? Well, you can have that if you truly understand your righteousness. If you understand who you REALLY are in Christ, you won't even have to think about self-esteem. How you view yourself will be perfect, because Christ is perfect! Jesus didn't walk around wondering what people thought of His message, or His delivery, or His outfit or hairstyle. He didn't care who didn't approve of Him, or who ignored Him. He got spat on and crucified, and STILL PRAYED FOR HIS ENE-MIES. Do you remember His prayer while He was on the cross? He asked God to forgive the people that were beating and murdering Him. THAT'S the kind of love we can walk in, but we must first start with understanding our righteousness.

What is righteousness?

Righteousness, simply put, is being in right-standing with God, free from guilt or sin. Let's break this definition down a bit more. What is right-standing? It paints a picture of standing before God, and everything about you is "right." It's good. It's PERFECT. When we are free from guilt and sin, we are not just forgiven, but we are free of

50

the consequences of sin. Any problems or issues that have been caused by your own personal sin or others sinning against you, no longer affect you. You are COMPLETELY FREE from guilt and sin and its residue! This is righteousness.

How do I receive righteousness?

Believers receive righteousness from Jesus Christ. 2 Corinthians 5:21 says, "For He (God) made Him (Christ) who knew no sin to be sin for us, that we might become the righteousness of God in Him (Christ)" (NKJV; emphasis added). It says right there in that scripture that we are the actual righteousness – or right-standing with God – of God Himself. This means that we have the same standing with God that He has with HIMSELF. Now, I don't know everything, but one thing that I do know is that God has a pretty high opinion of Himself. He is perfect. And the only judge that can call Him perfect is God Himself, so God is perfect in His own eyes. What this means is that if this scripture is right (and it is), then God sees us as just as perfect as he sees Himself. Christ's perfect righteousness is applied to imperfect humans; therefore, we can stand before God just as perfect

51

as Christ. Now you just need to believe it. Like, REALLY believe it. You need to put your FAITH in the righteousness that you are (or have) because of Christ.

If you want to fill your righteousness-faith-pocket (remember the forgiveness-faith-pocket we discussed in chapter two), to truly grasp and make your righteousness part of your identity, you can read the prior paragraph out loud for about three weeks (The one that starts with "Believers receive righteousness..." and ends with, "...because of Christ"). When you feel like it's really in you, just continue to speak the Word over yourself. Simply say, "I am the righteousness of GOD, in Christ."

When I got a revelation of my righteousness, I was never the same. I am in the SAME position as Christ. Just as good as He is.

Okay, so how does righteousness apply to my married life?

Truly understanding your righteousness not only makes it difficult to be offended, but makes it EASY to walk in love, both of which are especially important in marriage. Perfect love never gets offended - NEVER.

That means that no matter what your husband says to you, or how he treats you, you never feel hurt, angry or resentful toward him. This sounds almost impossible, right? Albeit a seemingly unattainable goal, this is the goal that the Lord asks us to strive for: perfection. Even if you're not even close, if you have this perfect love in sight as your end goal, I can guarantee you growth, just as the Word says.

> *But we all, with unveiled face, beholding as in a mirror the glory of the Lord, are being transformed into the same image from glory to glory, just as by the Spirit of the Lord.* (2Corinthians 3:18 NKJV)

When you look in a mirror in this natural realm what do you see? An exact image of yourself. Why? Because that's who you are. In this scripture, it is saying that when you take the veil off and can see the REAL you, what you see looking back is the glory of the Lord. This is another iteration of how our righteousness works. If you are in Christ Jesus (righteous), then when you look in the "mirror," you should see God.

> *We are all a work in progress, but the end goal that we should all be working toward is perfect love.*

Now, although we have been made perfect through Christ, we are humans with obvious weaknesses and imperfections. God knows this about us and knew that there would be a need for growth. This is why, in the second half of this scripture, it says that we are being "transformed." It says that we will go from glory to glory; we experience our transformation in levels of glory. This is true with our *love skill level* as well. For example, we may go from only knowing about love, but still finding ourselves angry with others on a daily basis, to the next level of understanding forgiveness and trying to be more patient. The next level of glory concerning our love walk might be that we are patient almost all of the time with most people, but still struggle a bit with our loved ones – able to forgive them, now more quickly. If we decide that perfection is our goal, then in theory, our skill level concerning our love walk would increase greater and greater, until we could walk in *perfect love*: the kind of love that doesn't even need to exercise forgiveness, because it is impossible to offend.

When we understand our righteousness, our love walk comes more easily. Without an understanding of righteousness, we put our value or self-esteem, in what we can or cannot do, what we think we are or aren't, or in the opinion of others. Let's take Gina, for example:

Gina is well-educated, intelligent and successful. She is under 30 years old and has climbed the corporate ladder to VP of business development in a Fortune 1000 corporation. This is all she's ever wanted, and she is living her dream of "success." Gina has based her self-esteem on the corporate successes that she has achieved. It's how she internally defines herself. Now another woman, Tiffany, gets hired in Gina's division to help "make some changes." The bosses say she has a "fresh, new perspective." Tiffany is a threat and makes Gina doubt her abilities, intelligence, job security, and in turn, who she is as a person. Gina's identity is threatened, and she begins to behave differently than she normally would toward Tiffany AND toward her other co-workers. She starts treating people badly – assuming they were out to get her or steal her position, not having her best interest in mind. She is behaving in a way that is out of character, because until now, her character had not been shaken. Gina seems to have become an entirely different person, for the worse.

Eventually, Tiffany swoops in and replaces Gina in her job. Gina's world has been turned upside down. SHE'S supposed to be "the best." That's what she identifies with – It's her IDENTITY. If someone else is better than her, then she doesn't know who she is anymore. She goes into a deep depression, causing her to spiral downward. Gina doesn't even try to look for a position at another corporation and eventually comes to financial and mental ruin.

This is an extreme case, but what if your self-worth and identity are not found in Christ? What if they are found in your intelligence, your beauty, your ability to be domestic, or even cook better than everyone else?

> *When I got a revelation of my righteousness, I was never the same. I am in the same position as Christ. Just as good as He is.*

The moment that anyone challenges one of these perceptions that you have of yourself, you feel they are attacking who you are as a person. It may not cause you to come to ruin, but it can be a huge hit on your worth as a person, as a woman and as a wife. This is why who you are (your identity) must be based in what Christ did for you.

The same way that improper self-esteem can be based on what one perceives they possess (special abilities, talents, a sense of humor, etc.) it can also be based on what they feel they lack. Some examples of this are: lack of talent/gifting, the inability to speak eloquently, negative body image, being too shy, the inability to rise above the level of the environment in which they were raised and all-around unattractiveness. When someone has improper self-esteem based on a negative self-image, it causes them to be preemptively defensive. This kind of person can be very difficult to be in close relationship with. At times they can be difficult to be around at all. Let's take a look at Kelly:

Kelly was a beautiful girl, but had always been a bit bigger than the other girls in school, making her self-conscious. As she grew into adulthood, she gained more weight, and instead of embracing the size she was (or even at least coming to terms with it), she adopted a negative self-image, always trying to lose weight, but never being able to keep it off. When she was younger, she was made fun of pretty regularly; but she didn't do much to stick up for herself. She had always naturally had an outgoing personality, but felt stifled in her school years as a result of pain and rejection. As she became an adult, she decided she wasn't going to let "haters" quiet her down anymore, and she decided to be the opinionated, outgoing person that she was born to be.

Unfortunately, her improper self-esteem misdirected this otherwise fun and exciting personality. She would wear what she wanted, go where she wanted and "not care what people thought", or this is what she would tell herself. The problem is that when your identity is based on a negative view of yourself, you really do care what people think.

One day, Kelly walked into a restaurant with a friend, talking loudly, and was dressed loudly as well. She was wearing a fuchsia blazer with a very colorful maxi dress. Kelly had always been noticeably pretty and that day she looked quite fashionable. She immediately noticed a couple of ladies in a booth looking at her and talking, as if they were talking about her, and assumed that they were judging her for her size, clothes, and overall appearance. This was common practice for Kelly, because despite her overall beauty, she was completely insecure and was constantly looking for someone to disapprove of her appearance. She was LOOKING for rejection. She sat down to eat, keeping a watchful eye on the ladies at the booth for any looks of disapproval, or glances they might cast her way. Kelly assumed their conversation was about her and her "garish" appearance. After almost an entire meal of this, Kelly had had enough. She got up, walked right over to their booth and said, "Do you have a problem with what you see? Would you like me to pose for a picture so you can just discuss me all day and STOP STARING?!"

Kelly was right. They had been noticing her, and even discussing what she was wearing that day. Linda, who was sitting in the booth facing Kelly, was also plus-sized and had been needing a pink blazer to go with some cool slacks she had recently bought. She noticed Kelly's sharp blazer as soon as she walked in the room and just knew it would work for her. At first Linda was trying to see if she could figure out where Kelly had gotten the blazer, but when she could not, had been discussing with her friend whether or not Kelly would mind if she inquired about the cute couture.

When you are always looking for rejection, you will consistently find it, whether it's an oversensitivity to normal human interaction, imagined, or even if you have to back someone into a corner to force them to reject you. Kelly didn't even entertain the idea that their conversation concerning her was positive. She walks around convinced that people disapprove of her and have a negative pre-judgment of her. Not only will it be difficult for her to find love with this kind of chip on her shoulder, but if she does find it, Kelly will have no problem making him miserable. Unless she heals in this area, Kelly will constantly be requiring her mate to convince her that he still approves of her and loves her. It will never work, because internally, she is already convinced that he doesn't. Self-hatred, self-doubt, and an overall bad self-image will lead to self-sabotage in relationships.

Consider the difference in effect that improper self-image and proper self-image has

> *Self-hatred, self-doubt, and an overall bad self-image will lead to self-sabotage in relationships.*

on your marriage. A bad self-image *alone* can destroy your entire relationship, even without the help of financial pressures, children, in-laws and career related issues. **If you don't want to be a party to ruining your marriage, you MUST invest time and effort into truly understanding your identity.** The image you have of yourself (self-image/self-esteem) MUST be found in Christ. Getting the true revelation of your righteousness into the core of your being is well worth the time and effort. God wants to replace your ashes with beauty (Is. 61:3). The opinion that we have of ourselves, whether it be positive or negative, is ashes compared to the beauty and perfection of God's opinion of us. Once we truly believe it, we become more beautiful, more attractive to everyone around us...Including our mate.

Chapter 4
Don't Be Eve

Throughout time and even in the Bible, some of the world's greatest manipulators were women. Now don't get all excited. I'm not saying that women are manipulators, or that we are even more apt to manipulate. I'm just saying that we're better at it. Women are powerful and influential (and pretty awesome, if I may say so myself). Women can be especially influential to their husband, particularly if he is a good man who respects his wife. Let's take a quick look at some of the most influential women in the Bible.

First, we have Sarai, who initially laughed at Abram when God told him that she would bear a child in her extremely old age. She eventually talked him into conceiving a child with her servant, almost directly in opposition with the promise and blessing of God.

It was Jezebel's influence that pushed her husband, King Ahab to worship and serve Baal, and essentially caused spiritual and moral disintegration for the whole of the Hebrew people.[1]

Lastly, there's Eve. Through her influence came the fall of all mankind. Something from which we were never quite able to recover. Yes, through Jesus Christ we are saved and have the victory against satan, but the sinful nature with which man is now born came as a result of Eve's influence, and consequently, Adam's sin, ultimately necessitating the need for a savior. Eve herself may not have been able to make all of man fall, but she took the fruit ("...of the tree of the knowledge of good and evil..."), ate it, and then gave it to her husband to eat, thus influencing the cause of the fall of mankind, male and female (Gen. 2:17-3:19).

Let's talk about Eve some more. There are so many things I find interesting about their story, especially in reference to the husband-wife relationship. I'd like to contend a few of them to you right now:

1. **Eve had to trust that her husband heard from God.**

   Then the LORD God took the man and put him in the garden of Eden to tend and keep it. And the LORD God commanded the man, saying, "Of every tree of the garden you may freely eat; but of the tree of the knowledge of good and evil you shall not eat, for in the day that you eat of it you shall surely die." And the LORD God said, "It is not good that man should be alone; I will make him a helper comparable to him." And the LORD God caused a deep sleep to fall on Adam, and he slept; and He took one of his ribs, and closed up the flesh in its place. Then the rib which the LORD God had taken from man He made into a woman, and He brought her to the man. (Gen. 2:15-18, 21-22, NKJV)*

We see here that God spoke to Adam, giving this warning directly to him, not to Eve. He couldn't have told

Eve not to eat of the tree (except to the extent that Eve was technically "inside" of Adam when God spoke to him) as Eve had not yet been formed. When Eve came, Adam must have told her the garden rules that had been set forth by God, their creator, Father, and the Maker of the Universe. *Eve had to trust that Adam heard from God.* There will be times in your marriage that you will have to do the same, even in the midst of conflicting evidence from outside sources.

2. satan (the serpent) knew to go through Eve to attack Adam.

Now the serpent was more cunning than any beast of the field which the LORD God had made. And he said

What if Eve had made the right choice?

to the woman, "Has God indeed said, 'You shall not eat of every tree of the garden'?" And the woman said to the serpent, "We may eat the fruit of the trees of the garden; but of the fruit of the tree which is in the midst of the garden, God has said, 'You shall not eat it, nor shall you touch it, lest you die.'" Then the serpent said to the woman, "You will not surely die. For God knows that in the day you eat of it your eyes will be opened, and you will be like God, knowing good and evil." (Gen. 3:1-5, NKJV)

At this point, Eve had a choice. She could trust her husband, and that he had heard from the Lord, or she could believe this source who seemed to know what he was talking about. What the serpent said to her sounded reasonable and intelligent. He seemed confident and wise, so she thought on this new information for a bit. satan knew that in order to get to Adam, who had heard directly from the Lord, he needed to go through Eve. In this moment it was of utmost importance for Eve to have trusted in her husband, but instead she let the enemy deceive her. satan will absolutely try to get to your husband through you. He knows how much influence you have over him, and that with just a few words, you can change his direction. It is up to you to resist him.

3. Eve thought she was doing something good.

So when the woman saw that the tree was good for food, that it was pleasant to the eyes, and a tree desirable to make one wise, she took of its fruit and ate. She also gave to her husband with her, and he ate. (Gen. 3:6, NKJV)

As women, we have been created to be wise and discerning. Part of the attributes God gave us to make us a suitable "helpmeet" for man is that we can see into situations. We can often discern when something may go wrong, or when something "just isn't right." God made us wise. He made us careful and He made us caretakers, so that we would look out for those around us, including our husband. There is something in your husband's heart that knows this, and *wants* this from you, so he is often receptive to it. It is because of this dynamic that we must be careful not to be deceived by the enemy or his logic. Certain things may *make sense* to you as a wise woman, but as a godly wife, you also have an obligation to stay in faith and believe the Word of God FIRST. There is a perfect mix that can come only from the Lord. Pray for discernment in all situations, and always be careful to hear God's voice and follow His leading in these situations. In those times when your husband hears from God on behalf of both of you, you believe it with him!

Please don't misunderstand what I'm saying. I don't believe that only the man must hear from God for the family. We have full capability to hear from God as women. All throughout the Bible there are female prophets and references to women prophesying and hearing directly from God. What I am saying is this: What if Eve had made the right choice? What if, instead of listening to the crafty "voice of reason" (the serpent), she decided to believe what Adam told her God had said? What if she shut the serpent down, rebuked him and sent him out of the garden?

Now I ask you: What kind of wife do you want to be?

Check Your Motives

With just a few words, you can greatly influence your husband. This can actually feel kind of nice – powerful even – to a woman, but that's just the thing: You ARE-powerful. It is for this reason that you must be so

69

careful. A discerning wife will watch her words. One of the best ways to begin doing this is to constantly check your motives. It is nearly impossible for someone with truly pure motives to be an evil influence. Sometimes we have clear ulterior motives, like when you start discussing a surplus in the bank account because you've been eyeing a new dress. At other times our motives may be hidden.

One example of hidden motives can be from a root cause of bitterness. When you have a root of bitterness in your heart as a result of unforgiveness toward someone, it can show up in numerous, ugly ways. Let's take a woman, for example, who grew up with an absentee, "good-for-nothing" father:

Aisha did not have her dad at home. She grew up with her mom and two older sisters in the house, and mom made it no secret that as soon as Aisha was born, dad was out of there. He left and he barely ever came back, except when he needed something from mom, like a bed to sleep in or some money to "hold him over" until he got paid from the next job. Mom raised her daughters to hate their father. She only spoke negatively of him, berating him when he was around and harshly criticizing him and his character as a man and a father.

Without realizing it, Aisha grew up learning to hate men. To her, subconsciously, they were the enemy. Of course, she didn't realize this because she WANTED a man. She thought she loved men, because she had the natural desire that most women have to be with one.

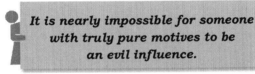

It is nearly impossible for someone with truly pure motives to be an evil influence.

She had romantic feelings for men, and would even become easily infatuated, wanting to spend as much time as possible with them and liking many of the characteristics of her boyfriend at any given time.

What Aisha didn't realize was that she had deep seeds of hatred toward men that had been planted by the absence of her father and fertilized by the words *of her mother. This resulted in roots of bitterness and a great need for inner healing.*

Fast-forward to five years into her marriage, we find that Aisha had been making her husband, Anthony, pay for the trespasses of her father. She had made him the enemy, and at this point they were engaged in war. He was not near perfect, but no matter how hard he tried, she gave him no grace. To Aisha, every mistake he made was a direct assault on her. Every time he came home late from work, she made serious accusations. He couldn't even mention wanting to hang out with his buddies without Aisha accusing him of not loving or liking her enough, and even of wanting to leave his family. **Tony was a normal man, behaving like a regular human being, but to her, his every day actions were an all-out assault on her.**

At the same time that Aisha WANTED Tony to want her and love her, she was EXPECTING him to do wrong by her. This created a twisted motivation in almost all of their important conversations. She was constantly trying to catch him in the act of something.

Her motive was never love. It was fear. Aisha was fully motivated by the fear that Tony would use her and then abandon her and their children. When this fear is the driving force behind most of your conversations, you can't have a healthy relationship, you can't build someone up to do better, and you certainly can't walk in the love (toward your spouse) that God has called you to.

We talked about the importance of forgiveness and healing in chapter two but sometimes we aren't aware of our broken places. (For more information on this, see my book *How to Be Whole*, 2017.) This is why I say the following prayer from Psalms on a regular basis. I suggest you pray this scripture *every day*, until you feel the paradigm shift that comes when your motives begin to become purer.

Search me, O God, and know my heart; Try me, and know my anxieties; And see if there is any wicked way in me, And lead me in the way everlasting. (Ps. 139:23-24)

When you begin to renew your mind with the Word of God (Rom.12:2), at first you may feel no change, but don't give up. It's a process. Initially, after your spirit begins to convince your mind a bit, you may say something that

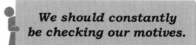

We should constantly be checking our motives.

you would normally say and then catch it afterward. Perhaps you would then apologize or attempt to repair the damage. With a bit more convincing (building greater faith in this area), you might catch yourself mid-sentence, then stop and redirect your message to your husband. Before long, you will think before you speak, which is a very powerful place to be. The Bible tells us to be "...quick to listen, slow to speak and slow to become angry," (James 1:19, NIV). This allows us to stop and think about the consequences of our words and the effect they will have on those around us. Then we can carefully craft the proper words to speak, with pure motives and out of the best intent.

Consider the powerful, positive influence you can be over your husband if you are consistently choosing your words carefully, and with the purest, godliest, most loving motives. The final and highest goal is to be able to pour out from a place of purity. We should always be slow to speak, but the place we want to get to in this journey of "pure motives" is where whatever is coming out of us is *naturally* coming from a pure place. As you build your faith for purity and openly let God do a work in you to rid you of any fearful, anxious or even "wicked" place, what will be left will be only what God has planted.

This journey may be simple for some, but for most, it will not. When you ask God to show you any "wicked" (crooked or twisted) way in you, He will. Some things from your past might be brought up that you've suppressed or have even forgotten about, but it's still affecting your relationships today. There may be things that are difficult and tedious to face, but it's worth it! It's time to be free of the ties that bind. Jesus is the yoke destroyer and the burden remover! He will disconnect you from unhealthy ties you have to your past, including those hurtful people and the negative emotions they've caused. I encourage you to face this head-on, and invest the necessary time and effort it takes to get completely freed and healed from past hurts. It's an investment in your future happiness and your future relationships.

Some Final Words About Motives

We've learned that we must desire a pure heart in order to have pure motives, and even talked about one technique we can use to purify our heart. This prayer is a way that we can become aware of the baggage that we carry from our past: baggage that can affect the way we approach our mate and our relationship. We must, however, remember that there is always maintenance.

We can buy a new car or even a used car that has been completely tuned up with a fresh paint job and all new fluids, plugs, brakes & tires, but that's not the end of

> *Doing the right thing with the wrong motive is still the wrong thing.*

it. We all know that we need to bring it into the shop regularly for maintenance, repairs, fluids, etc., or else it will begin behaving badly. Its behavior will begin to deteriorate, and it will no longer be at its peak performance. It's the same way with motives. We should constantly be checking our motives.

If you are praying for God to search you and show you anything that needs to be eliminated, then a whole lot does not need to be said on this topic. You want a clean heart; you don't want to use the influence you have over your husband to manipulate him. You want to be careful that you are motivated from a pure heart and by the spirit of God. But just like a vehicle needs maintenance to continue to operate at peak performance, you need to see to it that you consistently maintain a pure heart and pure motives. This will allow you to operate at your peak performance as a wife. I cannot express to you how important it is to have the desire for a pure heart in marriage. You should seek hard to attain this goal throughout all of your relationships. You can do the right thing, but doing the right thing with the wrong motive is still the wrong thing.

Commit today to letting your inside match your outside, and seek to desire what GOD desires for your husband, as opposed to what you desire for him. Become a wife who trusts God wholly and completely with her husband and has pure and loving motives. If you do this, you will find that, in the end, God has given you the things that you have so longed for in your marriage.

Chapter 5

Letting Him Off the Hook
Let him be an imperfect human

The Bible does tell us to patiently persevere toward completion; to grow and mature, striving toward perfection (James 1:4). But let's face it: Most of us just aren't there yet. Jesus is the only man who was ever perfect. Your husband (or future husband) is not perfect, your parents weren't perfect, and you certainly aren't perfect. And guess what: That's okay! Smile! We're all beautifully imperfect together! The Bible says that all have sinned and fall short of the glory of God (Rom. 3:23, NIV). So it is confirmed: You can expect your husband to have faults and weaknesses. To fall short, just like all of us... Including yourself.

This all sounds so reasonable, doesn't it? However, you wouldn't believe the number of complaints I get from women about their husbands, for being normal, faulted human beings. **Many times we are willing to accept imperfections and faults, even sins, from our spouse, but not if they're ones that we don't identify with, ourselves.**

The philosophy might look like, "Of course my husband is not going to be perfect! I'm aware of that. He just can never lie to me." Well, what if lying is the sin he struggles with? What if it's the weakness he faces? You may think it's okay to gossip and say negative things about other people,

> *You can expect your husband to have faults and weaknesses. To fall short, just like all of us... Including yourself.*

and would actually be just fine with him doing the same, but his lies are unacceptable? Is one sin greater than the next? This is a powerful concept, because it not only makes us take a look at ourselves, and our own ways, but it causes us to have to accept the very different faults of others.

It is biblical for us, as the body of Christ, to strengthen one another if we are weak or if we fall. I have had numerous women come to me about their husband's lies. They are fed up and don't want to deal with it anymore, but I ask, "have you considered the cause?" In the beginning of the marriage, what kind of consequences did they face when they mustered the courage to "fess up" to the truth? Were they punished for the truth, and then repeatedly punished until they were literally trained to lie? Or perhaps it was their childhood. When they got in trouble for doing the wrong thing, was the consequence abusive or unbearable for them? Now don't misunderstand me. Lying is absolutely not okay, and this behavior should be corrected. But these are things that we should know about our significant other. If a lie keeps one safe, they are more likely to do it. The definition of this "safety" can be different for different people, based on their greatest emotional needs. Safety for one man is acceptance and approval. For another, it might be a peaceful home and family life. Each and every one of us are so different, but **we need to be willing to understand and accept our differences, and continue to respect each other as men and women of God, despite our many flaws.**

Lying is just one example of a flaw or weakness that you may not directly identify with, but I can promise you, there are many others, you may encounter throughout your marriage. To name a few, there's also la-

> **We need to be willing to understand and accept our differences, and continue to respect each other.**

ziness, impatience, harshness (or rough speaking), the tendency to be late, overly critical, judgmental, being a workaholic and even not caring enough about appearance can really irk some women. This is where the relationship and what is expected of you can get complicated. However, if you can catch the revelation of love, and master it, you can have a healthy, biblical, thriving marriage.

This is especially key for women, because we are awesome. Because of our awesomeness, we can tend to be a bit harder on our men. *However, if you can use this God-given power of awesomeness to give you the strength to put the following principles into action, you will be able to respect your man appropriately and cover him with God's perfect love.*

There are three scriptures that complement each other perfectly to teach us how to approach the issue of having an imperfect, human husband:

1. Eph. 5:33, NKJV
Nevertheless let each one of you in particular so love his own wife as himself, and let the wife see that she respects her husband.

"But I don't feel like my husband is loving me properly. How can I be expected to *respect* him?!" First, I must point out that the scripture does not say, 'and IF he loves her properly, see that she respects her husband.' In every case in the Word of God, when we are commanded to behave in a certain way, it is without stipulations. God wants us to love others, whether or not they deserve it. He even commands us to love our enemies! This tells us that no matter how our husband is behaving, if he is our husband, we are to respect him. Again, this sounds difficult - because it is! But if you understand what the Word of God says about it, it can be easier. After all, we are imperfect ourselves, but it doesn't mean that we don't also expect love and respect from our spouses, does it?

Think of any imperfections you may have. Now, do you think that it would be fair to let your husband off the hook from loving and respecting you just because you don't behave perfectly as a wife? Let's say you were just messy. You leave messes all around and don't clean up after

> *No matter how our husband is behaving, if he is our husband, we are to respect him.*

yourself. You leave your clothes on the floor for him to pick up and your dirty dishes spread all over the kitchen for him to clean up, wash, dry and put away. Is this behavior acceptable? Absolutely not! It's rude, inconsiderate, and disrespectful to everyone who walks through your home. Does it give your husband a license to be unloving toward you? No way! He has been commanded by the Word of God to love you the same way Christ loved His people, the Church (Eph. 5:25). He must therefore love you unto "death" (implying great sacrifice), regardless of your unacceptable behavior. So in the same way, regardless of his behavior, we are to respect our husbands: outwardly and in our hearts.

Pray for him.

The second scripture I want to mention in the trilogy relates to the solution. It is always helpful in our situation to know that there is light (hope) at the end of the tunnel.

2. 1 Cor. 13:7, NKJV
(Love)...bears all things, believes all things, hopes all things, endures all things.

"What do I do if I am trying my best to respect him, but I still feel that I NEED for him to change his behavior?" You pray for him, while BELIEVING THE BEST IN HIM.

This scripture is telling us how to love. Part of loving is bearing and enduring "all things," including his behavior, while still believing "all things." This "all things" refers to believing the best in him; believing that he WILL

behave in a way that is acceptable to you. **You must believe the absolute best in your husband as you pray
for him. Have complete faith that he will be every bit
of the man of God that The Word says he is.** As you
pray, you must BELIEVE (and stay in faith) that he is
even now being perfected by The Word, and that he WILL
tell the truth at the next opportunity that he has to lie.

As you are praying for your husband, you must forgive him (Mark 11:25). Remember, forgive him over and
over again, even for the same offense (Matt. 18:22), or
you can render your prayer ineffective (Gal. 5:6).

A Note on "Nagging"

Do not complain to him about the problem. Tell him
once. He probably already knows anyway. My husband
once told me that after I have told him something for the
third time (pointed it out once, reminded him twice), it
was nagging. I have held on to that since then because **I
don't want to make my husband feel as if I think he
is too incompetent to get my message the first (or
even second) time.** Now, if I decide to tell him something a third time, I am making a conscious decision to

86

make him feel NAGGED. I don't know about you, but I don't want that reputation. **I want my husband to feel that everything I say is important, and if I use up my opportunities on complaining, degrading, or repeating my concerns about him, eventually I will dilute the importance of my words, in his opinion.** As a result, he will start to listen less closely, rendering my opinions less and less important and impactful to him. In the end, I will lose his respect.

After you have stated your concern once or twice, and he doesn't change, pray for him, believing that he will change, forgiving and staying in faith for your husband. You will see change. God can change the heart of a king.

What does "The Covering Love" look like?

3. Col. 3:13, NLT

Make allowance for each other's faults, and forgive anyone who offends you. Remember, the Lord forgave you, so you must forgive others.

Oh, how I love this third scripture! At this very point in my life, as I write this book, this is my FAVORITE scripture! The reason? Because I live by this. For so long, I had a bit of doubt in myself that I was too easy on people, or that I "allowed too much." I would see some others be so hard on people and their sins and faults, and I felt like maybe I was soft, but this verse set me free! It speaks to the fact that God foreknew that people were not going to live up to our standards; that they would have faults. So He knew that He needed to give us direction on what to do about it: "Make allowance." We are SUPPOSED to make allowances for each other's faults! What does this mean?

You must believe the absolute best in your husband as you pray for him.

One simple example would be, if your husband habitually got home later from work than he told you he would. Instead of complaining and/or being angry every time it happened (almost daily), you could make allowances, or provisions. If you are the one who cooks dinner in the evenings, and he loves to come home to a hot meal, his lateness could potentially cause a problem. How do you make an allowance for this?

First, you must stop looking at this as him lying to you and as a personal offense on YOU. This is a self-centered (victim) and somewhat narcissistic attitude, and we seek to serve and be selfless, like Jesus, yes? So we should see this instead as a personal flaw that HE has. We look at this through the eyes of understanding. We say, "He's not lying to me to spite me. He just really doesn't know how long it takes for him to wrap up at work and get home."

Now that we know that he has this issue of perhaps not being a good judge of time, we ask ourselves, "How can I help my husband?" Instead of angrily packing dinner up and muttering negative comments about him as we are closing down the kitchen, we can lovingly make allowances or provisions for him. Ahead of time, we can say, "I know he thinks he'll be home at 6:30, but based on his usual timing, that means I'll probably see him around 7:15." What you might do is make him a plate, cover it, and leave it in the microwave.

Then you can set a nice place for him at the table, complete with a drink, and follow up with a loving text that says something like this:

> Hey Boo! I made u some yummy chicken & rice w/green beans (your fav)! It's all ready 4 u in the microwave when u get home. All u have 2 do is press start. I love u. Can't wait 2 C u soon 💜

"But Niki, just one verse ago, you said that we are supposed to expect the best in our husband. Doesn't doing this contradict our "believing the best?"

This is where it gets tricky. Exercising the truths in all three of these verses, simultaneously, takes maturity and discipline. On one hand, you want to expect the BEST and be able to pray in faith for the best from your spouse, but on the other hand, you must make an allowance that could be communicating the message that you think he probably WON'T come through on this. All the while, you need to continue to respect this person that seems to say one thing and do another. It all sounds a bit difficult and contradictory, right? It's not. It takes a

discerning, mature person to understand the wisdom of
The Word of God. We are to believe the best in our husband. When we are doing this, we are saying, "I believe
that you tell me the truth, and when you speak I believe

your words, and
that you have
the right heart,
and even that
you fully intend

> *God foreknew that people
> were not going to live up to
> our standards, so He gave us
> direction on what to do
> about it.*

to be home at the time you say. I'll even go so far as to
say that I believe you, when you say you WILL make it
home by 6:30 this evening. BUT in the case that you
don't, I will make sure that you are taken care of and
forgiven ahead of time."

This isn't contradictory. It actually reminds me of
three people: Shadrach, Meshach and Abed-Nego.

*If we are thrown into the blazing furnace, the God
whom we serve is able to save us. He will rescue us
from your power, Your Majesty.* [18] *But even if he
doesn't, we want to make it clear to you, Your Majesty,*

that we will never serve your gods or worship the gold statue you have set up. (Dan. 3:17-18)

These three young men had complete, unwavering faith that God would deliver them out of the blazing furnace, but then they said that even if God didn't do it, they still would NOT do the wrong thing! This is the principle we need to grasp onto here. **We are saying that, through faith in God, we believe our husband can do it and that he will; but even if he didn't, WE will not do the wrong thing.** We will forgive, choose to love and respect him, and make allowances for his faults, just as Jesus did over 2,000 years ago. He died to (save us and) forgive us, AHEAD OF TIME, for the sins we will commit tomorrow, next year, and for the rest of our lives.

This is being an amazing wife: Giving respect to a husband who doesn't deserve it, because GOD asked us to. And God asked us to, because He knew that our husband would need it. We'll speak more on respecting your husband in the following chapter.

Let him off the hook with his apologies

The purpose of this chapter is to help you understand how to not be so hard on your man. Growing to a full maturity and understanding of "the covering love" and marital respect can be a big undertaking, so I wanted to arm you with a few concepts and techniques to begin practicing, so you know what it means to cover your spouse.

One thing I really see women mess up on is accepting an apology. For a lot of men, "traditional" apologies just don't come easily. So as their spouse, we need to encourage them in this practice. We know that our spouse is not going to be perfect, right? But we would like them to be able to own up to their wrongdoings and apologize to us when it's called for. So why would we discourage this behavior? It would be like our child eating all of their green leafy vegetables, and then we scold them afterward for using a spoon instead of a fork. We want them to eat the greens, yes? It's good for their health. As a matter of fact, greens (like apologies) are good for everyone's health! I know it sounds ridiculous that a wife would discourage their husband from apologizing, but it happens so very often.

I have seen a husband do wrong and then, out of love for their wife, put down their pride and apologize, verbalizing their regret for what they've done. Instead of an "I forgive you" from their wife however, they get back a rant of agreement, renaming everything that was wrong with what they had done. For some, if they don't

> *We must give people the space to be themselves and do the right thing, THEIR WAY, no matter how well we know how to do it.*

get the play-by-play of the trespass from their spouse during an apology, they get scolded for the apology being too short. If your husband has done something wrong, and then says, "I'm sorry," your response should not be "For what?" (trying to draw more out of him, manipulating him into seeming more remorseful). You both know what it's for. **Don't be a jerk. Accept his apology and forgive him. Assume he means it. Give him the benefit of the doubt, because that's what love does, right?** If love "believes all things..." (meaning: believes the best in others) and you are walking in love as God has asked you to, then you believe that when your husband says he's sorry, he is sorry.

Whatever level of self-control it may take for you to respond with a simple "I forgive you," and perhaps a "thank you," exercise that self-control. Otherwise, you will be like the parent who reprimanded the child for doing the right thing, but not doing it just like you would. We must give people the space to be themselves and do the right thing, THEIR WAY, no matter how well we know how to do it. This brings me to my last point about letting a man apologize.

Everyone's apology will not look the same. As a matter of fact, your style of apology can be so different from your spouse's (or others, in general), that Gary Chapman actually wrote a book on it, called *The Five Languages of Apology*[1]. I highly recommend you add it to your "marriage library!" What you need to know is that the feeling behind it is the same. Whether we say, "I shouldn't have done that, and I apologize," or "I'm sorry. Is there some way I can make it up to you?" Or various other things we can say to communicate remorse and/or the fact that we desire to move on, it all means the same thing. Our part is simple: Let him off the hook, walk in love, accept his apology, and move on.

Chapter 6
Men Are Simple:
A Man's Three Basic Needs

**As originally taught
by Pastor David S. Winston...**

I believe that a man's 3 basic needs are food, sex (often), and respect. I believe that when none of these are forsaken, you will have a happy man. Giving a man all of these things says to him, "My wife really loves me." Conversely, when they are lacking, a man can feel neglected, not worthy, and unloved. When done correctly, a man can feel extremely valued by his wife, and feel like a valuable part of the marriage relationship.

Food is important because, well let's face it, most men like to eat... and eat well. Feeding a man's stomach with a good meal is like cuddling his soul. It makes us feel so good inside.

Sex is important because it keeps the marriage relationship healthy. As a man, there are some frustrations and imperfections in the marriage that can become completely blown out of proportion when sex is not happening. Lack of sex usually seems to amplify the "perceived" problems in a relationship for a man. I don't know of many men who are married, not getting sex, and think their marriage is wonderful. It just doesn't happen that way. Regular sex is a necessary part of a healthy marriage relationship.

Lastly, respect is the biggest, most important thing that you can give your man. It says that you love him and care for him. If you disrespect a man often enough, you will have a hard time convincing him that you love and care for him. When you include a man in on decisions, it says to them that you respect their opinion and position. Respect is how men interpret love. Respect what they say, respect them in how you treat them, speak respectfully to them, and respect them in how you talk about them to others (regardless of if he is in the room or not). Many men in unhappy marriages cite disrespect as a common cause for their unhappiness.

-Pastor David S. Winston

Men are simple. Even the most complex man can be broken down into some pretty basic categories when it comes to general, overall, marital bliss. The ideas outlined in this chapter may be difficult to master, and they may offend some of you, but what they will most assuredly do, is make a (good) man into a happy husband.

Since about 2009, I have seen my husband teach this to different groups, and I feel that the fact that

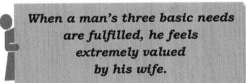

When a man's three basic needs are fulfilled, he feels extremely valued by his wife.

the message has continued to remain constant speaks to its accuracy. I do believe that my husband is a man of God, that he hears from God, and that he is humble enough to admit when he's wrong, and consequently, change his ways. In all my life, my husband has given me more respect than any other man, or even person that I've ever known (Of course he's given me love also, but I want to focus on the respect in making this point). That being said, what he is teaching here is not from a place of chauvinism, selfishness, or feelings of entitlement. Instead, it's out of an honest and genuine look at the delicate ego of the male man, and what we can do for him that makes him feel the most at ease, at peace and comfortable. Whether, as a woman, you like what I am saying in this chapter or not, I can say that we have tested this theory over the years, by way of our own marriage and by consulting with other men, and the agreement has been unanimous.

So here goes... If you want to make your husband (or future husband) happy, and even more importantly, happy that he married you, read on.

Note: We use the word husband very concretely in this chapter. Because sex is involved, and we believe that sex should be saved for the confines of marriage, this chapter refers very specifically to husband and wife.

A MAN'S THREE BASIC NEEDS:

1. Food

You may balk, you may get offended, you may laugh, but a man feels cared for when you feed him. Have you ever been in a room when a man found out that a woman can cook? Or better yet, a group of men? They get so excited! Those feelings are a clue to the genuine happiness that a man feels at the thought of a delicious, home cooked meal. I'm not going to go into the primitive roots or cultural background of this concept. There is much to be said for those, but that feeling you get when a man does something wonderful for you, that makes you feel so cared for, and at the same time you also happen to thoroughly enjoy (perhaps it's a clean car, buying you a new outfit, a handwritten poem all about how glorious you are, a relaxing massage, or a perfectly planned date) is almost the same feeling that a man gets when you take your time and energy to make sure he's fed. Except, in his case, he's also no longer hungry.

You may have heard the saying before: The way to a man's heart is through his stomach. If it weren't true, I wouldn't be pushing it so hard. There are so many reasons why this may be true, and you can think it's sexist and egotistical, but that won't help you "win" a man nor "keep him happy." When a woman can cook, it not only tells a man that he's going to be fed, hopefully for the rest of his life, but it also tells him that his family will be taken care of.[1] Essentially, it makes him feel like his future family is safe (Even more so if he cannot himself cook). When you think about it, that's beautiful. Don't you want the man that is wonderful enough to have earned your love to be able to share in that feeling? Doesn't he deserve to feel the warmth of knowing that you care about his stomach and satisfaction, and in turn, his well-being?

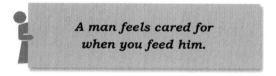

A man feels cared for when you feed him.

Let's follow this up with a few brief statements about food and your husband:

- **You don't need to be a master chef.**

Everyone has to start somewhere, so even if you're at the ramen noodles and grilled cheese stage, that's okay! It's the heart that counts, so be encouraged! We all improve with time at everything we do, so keep trying and eventually you will be an old pro.

At my first Thanksgiving dinner attempt, I left the plastic encased giblets in the turkey while it roasted, but eventually I learned that those get removed and we can even put them to good use!

If you want to gain more skill quickly, I highly recommend group cooking classes (Especially ones categorized by ethnicity, like Chinese, Italian, Indian – as opposed to very specific ones, like sushi, bread making, etc. Save the specific lessons for after you've learned the basics). There are also many books you can buy. The easiest and least intimidating are ones with lots of pictures (which can be very helpful), and that have the word "basic" in the title (e.g. Basic Italian, or the Basics of Soul-Food Cooking, etc.). If you prefer not to do either of those, or if money is an issue, try YouTube videos and follow cooking profiles on social media. Get it in front of you and start cultivating a "taste" for cooking.

- **You don't have to cook every night.**

You just have to make sure people are fed. I am at a place in my life right now where cooking six (or even four) nights a week is just not always possible. I do, however, take on the responsibility of feeding my family, and for this my husband is grateful. This doesn't even always mean that I actually GET the food.

In a normal week, I may cook three to four times, but one or two of them will be with the intent of food being left over for another night's dinner (or a weekend lunch). On Sundays, we eat out as a family, and then on another night or two we might eat takeout. Usually, I am the one responsible for getting the food to the table, but on the occasional day where I am not able to do everything in time, I will reach out to my husband and ask him to pick something up.

What you will not see me do (because it is unacceptable) is get so busy that I'm arriving home at 8:30 p.m. and haven't communicated about food to anyone. So what I mean about it being my responsibility is that whether it's through my own skill, going to a drive-thru, ordering delivery online, or asking my husband to take care of dinner, the feeding of my family is my responsibility. It is important to me that they are taken care of, and in turn, they feel cared for and loved.

- **If you CAN cook, but choose not to cook for him, this is like a slap in the face**.

Believe it or not, it can seem intentionally hurtful and uncaring. Why wouldn't you want to love him with your skills, your time, and your food? He deserves your best treatment. In all cases, including cooking, if you have the ability to do something that would make your husband feel loved, respected, and cared for, be like Nike, and just do it.

- **He will still love you if you don't cook, but he will wish you did.**

If a man had to choose between two almost identical women, but one could cook and the other could not, whom do you think he would choose? Enough said. If you don't already know how, learn how to cook.

2. Sex (Often)

Yep... Often. This is actually part of David's message. It is important to add that in there, because a wife should know that twice a year does not qualify as a sex life. If you are at that point in your marriage, your sex life is dead and needs resurrecting.

That being said, "often" is relative. For some it is every day, and for others it can be once every week or two. The main idea, however, is that sex, *often*, is important, especially to men. There really are two people groups that need to be separately addressed on this matter: the marrieds and the non-marrieds, because as the marrieds know, your concept of a "healthy sex life" changes after marriage. I will first write to the non-marrieds.

TO NON-MARRIEDS: I know you're probably excited and looking forward to the day when you can freely give your body to the man who loves and deserves you. Or perhaps you are nervous and apprehensive about that day. In any case, most times, our concept of what it will be like is usually not quite accurate. What we have come across most often in counseling pre-married (or engaged) couples is that they think they are going to be having sex far more often than they end up doing so. Although this is a common misconception, much disappointment, un-met expectations, and consequent feelings of rejection can be avoided if the proper expectation is laid out.

To engaged couples, I encourage good communica-tion, setting realistic goals, and definitely talking about your future sex life with a pre-marital counselor. Get perspective from someone who has been married (or has quite a bit of experience counseling married and en-gaged couples). Do not trivialize the importance of thorough, SAFE communication about sex and physical intimacy between a husband and wife. For some, it can make or break the marriage.

If you are a woman who is nervous or apprehensive about your impending sexual relationship, again I say, talk to someone. Specifically, a WOMAN who is very comfortable speaking on the subject (not your mom!), and have the

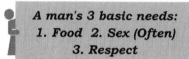

A man's 3 basic needs:
1. Food 2. Sex (Often)
3. Respect

conversation in private, without your fiancé around. If this is newer for you, I can assure you that you will feel much more comfortable discussing what needs to be addressed while you are outside of his presence.

Lastly, I want to issue a strong warning: When it comes to sexual conversation, those who are not married must be extra careful. If you are trying to wait for marriage (and I will assume that you are), it can be somewhat difficult to open up that topic without awakening something sexually. To help avoid prematurely stimulating an area that you want to stay dormant (for now), try following a few simple rules:

1. ***Wait to talk in-depth about your future sex-life until two or less weeks before the wedding.*** This will give you less time to "dwell" on what you and your fiancé have discussed.

   I do, however, recommend having some kind of initial, less detailed conversation about sexual philosophy earlier in the relationship. Some couples find out AFTER they are married that one's beliefs about what's permissible in the marriage bed, and the approach that they should take toward sex, are very different than the other's.

2. ***When you DO discuss sex in detail, do it in a "safe" place.*** A crowded restaurant, coffee house, or even in a counselor's office is fine, but do not discuss sex alone on a couch at your fiancé's apartment. Also, after this discussion, don't plan on being alone together for a while (at least one to three days might be best). Basically, don't discuss sex and then give yourselves ANY opportunity for temptation. You can try out everything you've discussed AFTER you say, "I do."

3. **_Know when you ovulate_**. I could explain how to find out when that is, but there are actually apps and websites for that.

> **_Non-Marrieds:_**
> **_When you DO discuss_**
> **_sex in detail, do it in_**
> **_a "safe" place._**

Do your research and know. Our time of ovulation is the short period out of every month that we are able to conceive. Because God made us so wondrously, He also designed our sexual libido to increase during that time. If there was a time when, naturally, you were the most likely to make some bad sexual decisions as a single woman, this would be it. During the time when David and I were courting, when I was ovulating, I would try my best to cover up my body, put my hair up, wear little to no makeup, and stay as far away from David as I could, physically (without completely avoiding him, of course). I would also usually let him know because sexual purity was our goal as a couple. It helped him to know when I was possibly at my "weakest," so he could plan on being stronger for me at those times. Working toward purity as a team is always best!

TO MARRIEDS: Your husband deserves your sex. Even when you don't feel like it, even when you're tired, and even when there's so little time (1 Cor. 7:5). There are good reasons not to have sex, but if we are not careful, you will have more reasons not to, than TO have sex, and eventually there's little to none.

Think of it as a meal. If you knew that you and your husband both were hungry and needed a sandwich, but you were tired, what would you do? You would get up and go make that sandwich! The idea of getting yourself out of the chair or bed you were in to go prepare some food probably did not appeal. You most likely even thought about just sitting there and staying hungry; but you finally decided to get up and make it. It only took a few minutes, and afterward, not only was your husband grateful for the food, but you even enjoyed it yourself! In the end, you were both fed and glad you did it.

Sex is a lot like this example. You need to DECIDE that it's something you're going to do. It doesn't need to be romantic, or inspired, or even that great. Like the lunch meat and mayo sandwich only; it still feeds you. But you DO need to stay in the habit of doing it. If your marriage is sex-starved, other problems begin to become amplified, especially to your husband.

I will tell you something: Good sex will keep a man happy. You could be bad at a lot of other things, but if you are satisfying him sexually, he is a whole lot less likely to notice the negative. This is not an encouragement to ignore other areas of growth as a wife. Because of our servant's heart and our loving attitude toward our husband, we should always be looking to grow in areas that please him and make him feel cared for. However, I am telling you that until you are perfected, where you lack will be so much less noticeable to him if you are "blowing his mind" in the marital bed.

"But Niki, what do you mean by 'blowing his mind?' I'm not quite sure if I am "good" at sex or not." Well, I hope you're ready, because I am about to tell you the secret to being great in bed. WIVES, are you ready?

The Secret to Being Great in Bed,
FOR WIVES!

ENTHUSIAM. Yep... That's it. You don't need to know "tricks," or have all kinds of sexy lingerie, or even know all about his anatomy. Those things are good, and you should always be continuing to learn how to improve in safe environments. (Be very careful trying to get sexual information off the internet, or anywhere that is not a

> **When a man is sexually satisfied, he is a lot less likely to notice the negative.**

controlled environment. You can come across some pretty traumatizing images and information), but if you want your husband to think you're good, just be enthusiastic about making love to him.

If you have an attitude of sexual enthusiasm for your spouse, it permeates all areas of your sex life. You say yes more often, you are more open-minded and giving during the process, you will be happy to do it, and he will feel more sexually accepted by you and desirable to you. In turn, you will also be more sexually satisfied (as you will surely have better sex, more often), and will most likely feel more accepted by your husband.

What do I do if I'M not satisfied?

Communication, communication, communication! You MUST talk about what you want, sexually. There are rules, however to discussing sexual desires (better yet, UNMET sexual desires) with your spouse. A man's ego can be fragile, especially in this area: He wants this so badly, he would love for it to be low-pressure, and in the end, he really wants to please you. Sex is extremely important and sensitive for him, and many husbands put a lot of pressure on themselves for their marriage's sexual "success."

If you aren't satisfied in general or with one particular encounter, whatever you do, do not try to talk about the problem DURING sex or immediately afterward. If you need something to change immediately (there is discomfort, for example) ask for what you need. A simple request will do. This is not the time, however, to start talking about how he always does this and telling him that you don't like what he's doing. Simply ask something like, "Can we try this?" (and reposition, with a smile).

If you want something from your spouse, sexually, make requests. This should be your primary mode of sexual communication. Complaining, being upset, or with-

> **Communication: You MUST talk about what you want, sexually.**

holding sex should not be your response to a subpar or even bad situation. He loves you, and he wants to please you. He just needs to learn how. It may not happen overnight, but be patient and continue to make requests. Try not to make too many at once. You don't want to overwhelm him, or make him feel like something is wrong with him.

Let's use the sandwich example again: If he asked you to add some tomatoes to his sandwich this time, you would, probably happily, knowing that you're making it even better for him. You know that because he got something extra on there that he wants, he will be even more satisfied with his sandwich, right? And the next time you made him a sandwich after that, he could even request

115

that you try mustard instead of mayo. You wouldn't mind. You would just feel like you were doing something a little extra for your hubby!

But what if he started eating the sandwich that you had just so lovingly made him, and he was like, "Ugh, what did you put on this sandwich?! It's just NOT good." And you respond by saying, "Oh, I'm sorry! Would you like me to do something else?" He then replies, "No. I'll just get through this," but begins to look disgusted as he picks pieces of lettuce out of his teeth and drops them on the plate. You ask him, "Would you like me to make you another? I can start over." And, obviously irritated, he says, "You've done enough. I'll just eat this so we don't waste it. It's fine." Now, would you want to make him another sandwich tomorrow? Nope.

This is what we do to our husbands sometimes when the sexual experience isn't perfect for us! We are completely insensitive to what's going on in their heads and in their hearts. Ladies... WIVES... Women of God: We must do better. Be a sexual ENCOURAGEMENT to your husband. Ask, LOVINGLY, for what you want, and I promise, your sex life will be so much better, more ful-filling and more satisfying for you AND your husband!

A last note: Each of you deserves the other's sexual energy, so don't waste it elsewhere, or by yourself. Save it for your spouse only. If you are inclined to fantasize, it should be about your spouse, and the energy that you create in doing so should be directed toward him and not kept or used privately, for yourself. I am not speaking to everyone in this. If this pertains to you, you know who you are.

3. Respect

Nevertheless let each one of you in particular so love his own wife as himself, and let the wife see that she respects her husband. (Eph. 5:33, NKJV)

In chapter five, we discussed the importance of re-specting your husband, even when you don't see why he deserves it. In this chapter, we want to discuss WHY it's important, and some *How-Tos* for respecting your hus-band. I want to make this as easy for you as possible.

Love Vs. Respect

I find it so interesting and enlightening that the Word of God repeatedly tells husbands to LOVE their wives, but we ladies are directed to RESPECT our husbands. I like to call God "The Great Psychologist." He knows exactly how we're made, because He MADE us! Because of this truth, He also knows exactly what we need. I also find it interesting that many women seem to resist the idea of giving respect to her man (or husband).

> *God called us to respect our husband, so we do it as service unto God.*

This is especially the case when he has a particular behavior, or behaviors, that she doesn't approve of. She then may feel that she has a case to argue that he doesn't DESERVE her respect, but as we learned in Chapter five (*Letting Him off the Hook*), him being deserving is not the qualifier. God called us to respect our husband, so we do it as service unto God, because we want to love Him through our obedience (Jn. 14:21). Therefore, disrespect is simply not justifiable.

But why do many women seem to resist the idea of respecting their husband? I believe it's because they don't understand it. If it is repeatedly implied that we, as females, need love, I believe that it is also implied that we UNDERSTAND the need for love. We are great at loving our children, loving our families, and of course, loving our husbands. We, in turn, often expect that love to be reciprocated, and when it isn't, we can feel disappointed and rejected. The inherent NEED for respect, however, is not in most women. At least, not as strongly as it is in men. We are just not wired that way.

You can even see it in children. I have four beautiful children: three boys and one girl, and I can most undoubtedly tell you that despite all of their differences, my little girl came out of the womb DIFFERENT than all of the boys. It actually surprised me how different she was, even from birth. She was just more... feminine.

There is something about the innate difference between males and females that causes our greatest need from a spouse to also be so different. So again, I contend to you that we as women don't inherently identify with respect, because it is not naturally an essential need of ours. Because of this, we need some basic training.

Understanding Respect

You feel that you deserve the love that you so desire, correct? And even in those times when you feel like you don't really deserve it, wouldn't it be nice to still feel loved? If your husband never failed to make you feel loved, whether you were deserving of it or not, it would be wonderful! You would feel so safe and cared for in the relationship, wouldn't you? This is exactly how he feels when you treat him with respect. It communicates EX-ACTLY the same message. A man feels so safe and cared for when he is treated with respect by his wife. And when we feel safe, it is much easier not to be defensive or combative. Why fight or argue when you are completely safe? There is nothing to fight against. Emotionally and mentally healthy people just don't do this.

Think about it: When you walk in a dark alley or down a hallway where you think someone could attack you at any moment, you're automatically on the defense. In this situation, if someone raised an arm to high five another person, you would see it and be ready to block. In an unsafe environment, you're ready to defend. If you are on a battlefield and the enemy is running toward you, gearing up for attack, you are armed and ready for combat. But when you're in your living room, the doors are locked, the alarm is armed, and you're safely nestled on your couch, you feel safe. You're not preparing yourself with defensive measures. There's no weapon in your hand. You are at peace. Your husband will feel at peace when you act respectfully toward him, because he feels safe and cared for, and his needs are being met.

How do I respect my man?

Respect can come in many forms, but I'm going to speak simply and practically. For the most part, men are *doers*. They want to provide a service for you, and they want to solve your problems. The desire to provide for you is in their inherent nature, and they want to feel valuable. It is part of our job as a wife to see to it that they feel fulfilled in these areas. The following are some tips to laying the groundwork for a foundation of respect in the relationship:

• **Recognition and Praise:**

We can start here. To reinforce the good that they are doing (or at least intending to do), we should recognize the work they've done and praise them for it. Compliment their work, their effort, and even the fact that they did the thing that you are addressing. You could say something like, "I can't believe you fixed that chair! It had really been bothering me, and you took the time and effort to do it without me having to ask. You did such a good job! I can't even tell it was broken."

Even if they didn't do a fantastic job, or didn't do it exactly how you would have liked, recognize the work and the job that they DID do. This is not a time for criticism! If you want him to continue to do things for you, and more importantly, feel respected, do NOT point out the negative in what he has done. This is a "praise-only" situation. It is always important to use words that affirm your husband. Remember, it will benefit no one for him to know where he doesn't measure up.

- **Gratefulness and Thanks:**

Do not underestimate the power of a "thank you." It communicates not only gratitude for what was done (or said), but it implies approval from you, and that they did well. Say thank you as often as you can; and when you can,

> *It is always important to use words that affirm your husband. It will benefit no one for him to know where he doesn't measure up.*

be specific. My husband is out of state to speak to young people at a conference even as I write this paragraph, I actually paused my writing to text him and thank him for bringing the Word of God to people everywhere. You not only need to thank them for the things they do for you, but also for what they do for others. You can thank him for being a good man, a great example, a good father, for being careful, or for being fast or excellent at their job. You can thank him for serving others, for being a good provider, for accepting your friends, for any amount of housework he does and for anything you can possibly think of. I truly believe that you cannot thank someone enough. When you thank your husband, you add value to his life. The most important person in his whole life approves of him and values his contribution to the world and to his family. That is a very affirming feeling.

What if I've made him feel disrespected?

When a man is upset with his wife, you can almost always trace it back to a feeling of disrespect. Even if he has trouble verbalizing it, or even consciously understanding it himself, there is a root of disrespect at the base of virtually every single issue he has with you. If you live by this rule and then use the following advice on how to handle these situations, you can navigate through this type of conflict more skillfully, and in turn, much more easily. Let's look at an example:

You ask your husband for his input on something. He gives it. After some thought and a bit more research, you make a decision, but it was not congruent with the input that he gave you. Suddenly, he seems upset with you, and you don't really understand why. As a matter of fact, you thought he would be proud of you for going

the extra step and doing research on the matter in order to make an informed decision. After some
prodding, you find out that he is bothered that you
asked for his advice, but then did the opposite.

The best thing to do here is:

   a) Defend your position. You did your research, and
      in the end you made the right choice. He needs to
      recognize that and get over it.

   b) Apologize for disrespecting him. Tell him that you
      really do respect his opinion, in no way meant to
      disrespect him, and that next time you will be
      careful not to let this happen again.

   c) Ignore his mood. Eventually he just gets over it an-
      yway, and things go back to normal.

If you answered *b*, you were correct! This, ladies, is
the go-to script for fixing an upset (disrespected) man. If
you are highlighting, highlight it. If you're annotating,
note it; and if you're married now, or ever plan on getting
married, MEMORIZE IT. The following sentences are

golden! "Oh honey, I apologize if I disrespected you! I absolutely respect you and did not mean to make you feel like I don't. In the future, I will definitely be careful not to let this situation happen again. I think you give great advice and would not want to do anything to discourage you from offering your advice to me the next time."

Voila! You just went from your man feeling disrespected, to feeling *completely* respected and revered in about four sentences! If you don't believe me, try it! The next time he seems upset about something between the two of you, do your detective work, and try to boil it down to an instance where he could've felt disrespected. Did you criticize something he did for you? Did you undermine a discipline that he gave to a child or even a pet? Did you go back, after the fact, and "fix" something he did or said? Or, perhaps you did something yourself

> *Apologize for disrespecting him. Tell him that you really do respect his opinion, and in no way meant to disrespect him.*

that you had already asked him to do (because he was taking too long for you). Any of these instances, and more, communicate disrespect to a man, and need to be addressed. If you use a variation of that script, I can almost *guarantee* that the problem will be resolved in a fraction of the time it usually takes. This not only works on husbands, but it will work on your brother, your male boss, your guy friends and especially on your daddy!

The only caveat is you. Sometimes when our man is upset, it's hard for us as ladies to see past the fact that we feel attacked, and in turn, unloved. This is where self-control is of utmost importance. You must put down your emotions, gather all of your strength, and humble yourself for the sake of your spouse and your marriage. You can do it! It's hard, but once you taste the sweetness of rapid problem-solving (efficient communication), you will not want to go back to the long, exhausting arguments of the past. If I taught you nothing else in this chapter, please remember the "respect script" that you learned today. It's a lesson to last a lifetime.

SECTION 2
HOW TO WIN HIM

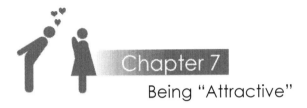

Chapter 7
Being "Attractive"

I could see how some might have an issue with this section, but hear me out first. I feel like there are so many valuable, amazing women out there that would make awesome wives, but because they are so busy being coy, or "guarding their heart" improperly that the men just can't see it. Or perhaps they're not busy at all - being shy and almost refusing to have conversations with men.

Take yourself, for example (if you are not currently married): You are investing time, effort, and energy into being an amazing wife by reading this book. I bet this is not even the first, nor the last thing you will do to invest in your future marriage. You are training yourself to be a skillful spouse, right? Well, what if you knew someone who was born with a natural gift and desire to sing? She seeks training by reading, taking voice lessons, practices technique, and becomes an amazing singer. Now, when it comes time to share her gift and she's asked to perform, what if she refuses? As a matter of fact, what if she never shares her gift? She's put all that thought, time, and effort into becoming a skillful songstress, and no one knows about it, because she won't put herself out there.

This is the problem I see: So many potentially great wives, wanting to be married, and even having an eye on someone, but refusing to "put themselves out there." I'm not saying to aggressively chase a man. There are, however, signals that say, "I'm approachable," or "I'm interested," or even "I know how to treat a man." This is in opposition to a lot of what I'm seeing women communicate. They seem to be saying, "Don't talk to me," "I don't need a man," and "If I got one, I wouldn't know what to do with him anyway."

Which one is you? Which one would you like to be? Well, if you want your "Boaz" to find you, fresh-faced and available, instead of having to unwrap layers of sack-cloth from your face, because you're looking like you're mourning, then read on for some tips, keys and general good-practices on "how to win him."

1. BE OPEN

This doesn't just mean to make yourself available, but you should be demonstrating fruit that communicates the covering love we talked about in chapter five. There are so many flawed men out there, but they know they're flawed...Just like YOU. We need to stop putting on this air that tells men that they need to work super hard to earn your respect, or that you have walls up that they need to break down before they can get in and get a glimpse of you. Men are attracted to someone who is understanding of others' faults, yet cares enough to be there for people anyway. If you seem like you are closed-minded or hard on people, a man will often back away. The man that chases you because he "likes a challenge" is not the man you want. You can't keep up playing hard-to-get over many years of marriage. It will prove to be exhausting for both of you, in addition to creating a constant atmosphere of strife.

Most people, including men, have insecurities. Don't you want a man who would cover your faults and flaws with love? Well, he wants the same. He wants to know that his heart will be safe with you and not under attack: That if he gets a little belly or doesn't earn as much money as *There are signals that say, "I'm approachable," or "I'm interested," or even "I know how to treat a man."* he'd like to, or that if he gets impatient at times, that you will be understanding and kind with him. Be that way now. If that's who you are, it's a great quality. Put it on display for all to see. After all, it looks like Jesus, and looking like Jesus draws men to salvation.

So I say to you: practice being open and kind hearted. Let it be part of you and part of your everyday life. Men will find you more approachable, and in turn, will approach you!

2. BE FEMININE

You want a man, right? Like, an ACTUAL MAN... Well, what if he dressed in women's clothing, acted like a lady, and to top it off, clearly had a female's hairstyle? Now,

I'm not referring to pop fashion, like high buns on attractive men, or even a man being a bit effeminate. I say to each his own with fashion trends and even attraction. I am referring to a man that often gets mistaken as a woman. One who is clearly trying to look like one and be perceived as "womanly." If you don't find that attractive in a man, my guess would be that men feel the same way about women who "seem" like men.

I did some interviewing of what I consider good, quality men for this portion of the book, and this was a common theme. I'm going to tell you what THEY said - in their words, not mine. I was told that a woman should not be bald (by choice), they should not wear all baggy clothes most of the time, and they should not be overly masculine. So the solution? Have hair, whether it be grown or purchased (but if it's purchased, let it be nice, feminine, non-intimidating, and not as STRANGE as you can get it, please), wear clothes that fit you, and be feminine. You're a woman. God made you that way, and you are BEAUTIFUL. See yourself as beautiful (as you truly are), and others will see you the same way.

3. CONSIDER YOUR PACKAGING

Now I'm not going to tell you to always wear skirts and curl your hair every day. It is very feminine and the many men would probably appreciate it, but not all of them. As the saying goes: different strokes for different folks. This is where I would say to take a strategic approach. Many of you don't need to change anything concerning your packaging, and I feel like you know who you are. If there is any doubt, then there may be room for development in this area.

In *considering your packaging*, I want to address four areas to evaluate. We will: **Consider him, consider ourselves, consider the pair, and then we will talk about what NOT to consider acceptable.**

You're a woman. God made you that way, and you are BEAUTIFUL. See yourself as beautiful and others will see you the same way.

Consider Him.

What does your ideal man look like? Is he a suited and booted business man? Is he a rapper? Is he an artistic type, or even possibly a minister? Does he workout a lot, or perhaps you like a man who loves to chill on the couch? There are so many "types" out there (people who possess particular characteristics that you are generally attracted to), and they say there's someone for everyone, so it's okay to like a certain type of guy (whether you will end up with whom you think you will, is another story). The difficult question to ask, however, is will HE like YOU? This is where our "packaging" comes in.

If you KNOW what you want, and it's a certain type, then you must ask yourself, "Am I what HE wants?" If you want an artist or a poet, consider what this type of man might be looking for. Do you even SOMEWHAT fit the mold? Lenny Kravitz liked Lisa Bonet. Not just because she was extremely pretty (probably my favorite female face of all time, outside of my daughter, Lily) but because she was what he was looking for. Whether he knew it or not, he was looking for like-kind. There is definitely the rare occasion where very different people are attracted to each other, but this is not the norm. In the case of personalities, opposites attract all of the time, but when it comes to lifestyle and major interests, most men will gravitate toward even their subconscious type. Lenny Kravitz approved of himself, and his identity enough to where he, at least subconsciously, wanted someone who reminded him of himself. If a man's self-esteem is properly intact, he will most often be attracted to someone he identifies with. *Are you her?*

Consider Yourself.

If someone is consistently attracted to others that have no resemblance to themselves, it can be a sign of an insecurity such as self-disapproval (or even self-hate), or baggage from their past. For example, a man who grew up with a mother who cared nothing about her looks or hygiene, can be so focused on finding a mate that cares supremely about her appearance that he's made that his number one priority, as opposed to something

> *If a man's self-esteem is properly intact, he will most often be attracted to someone he identifies with.*

more lasting and important. We must ask ourselves why we like what we like, and if perhaps it has to do with a crooked place in our heart such as insecurity or baggage. This is where the prayer from chapter four that I asked you to pray daily comes in. We want to be fully motivated from the right place. There's nothing wrong with having a type. We just want to ensure that it comes from a pure place and not from somewhere that could be destructive.

Consider the Pair.

Now that we've analyzed our desires in a man, let's get back to what he wants to see in you. Would a man who puts great emphasis on his appearance and fashion want a woman who wears frumpy, oversized t-shirts and old sneakers every day? Would a front-man in a rap group or band want a woman who never looks camera-ready? What about a minister of the gospel? Would he like his wife to look like she's always ready for a bath-room selfie, showing cleavage, midriff, and as much leg as possible? He shouldn't. So I encourage you to take a few minutes and envision the kind of man you want.

Then envision what kind of woman HE would want... Do you have some re-packaging to do?

Packaging ourselves the way our husband would like is not superficial or fake. It should come out of an attitude of serving one another. The man you end up with for the rest of your life is the man you're choosing to identify with. Your identities should be intertwined. When you marry, the two of you become one, right? Consequently, your exteriors should match your connected interiors.

Matching your husband does not have to be bondage, but you should desire to do so. Because you are selfless, you put him first and you want to serve him. It will please your husband if you put forth the effort in your appearance to look the way he likes you to look.

I'll use my husband and I as an example: I like to look "tough." When I met David, I had a LOT of big boots. Slowly, and over time, I relinquished my hold on most of them.

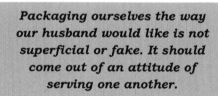

Packaging ourselves the way our husband would like is not superficial or fake. It should come out of an attitude of serving one another.

I now have one pair of clunky boots, and they are very much "statement" boots, so he understands the appeal. Still, I would not wear them on date night. David likes for me to look feminine and noticeable. I like to describe it as looking like a "pop star." He may not fully agree with the description, but for me, the more I feel like I look like a pop star, the more excited he seems to be about my appearance. Obviously, there is a time and place for everything, so I generally save that look for when it's appropriate, but I know what pleases my husband, and I aim to please. He even has certain preferences about my hair and make-up, and I try, most of the time, to serve him when it comes to this. When I go out without him (on my own, or with the children or friends), I allow myself to do what pleases me (or what's easiest, depending on the demands of the day), but when with him, I try to do what I know he will like. This is because I love him and want to serve him, selflessly, not because he puts any demands on me concerning my appearance.

The same goes for David. When we are going somewhere together, especially on a date, he asks me about what I would like to see him in. He has a desire to please me and make me happy, even my eyes, and I truly appreciate that he wants my input. It is an expression of his selfless attitude to serve me. Sometimes I give him no real opinion, and sometimes I do, but either way, I feel loved and served because he cares about my preferences.

Don't Consider These Okay.

The following is a list of some things that no man finds attractive:

- **Women who look crazy** ~ Wearing strange, extremely noticeable wigs or hairstyles (barring the current trends), carrying more than 3 bags at a time if you are not traveling or unloading your car, and sporting looks from three or more genres, simultaneously NEVER make you look like a sane person. (E.g. a church hat with a big fluffy cardigan sweater and old white sneakers – together)

- **Being completely age inappropriate** ~ There's room for a little leeway here, especially if you already have a younger or older look, or if you prefer a younger or older man, but you should NOT be 50, and wearing jeans that have words on both back pockets. If you're not sure if you dress age-appropriately, ask someone who's fashion choices you trust, and be humble enough to change.

- **Too many sparkles** ~ ...or make-up in general. Wearing too much make-up (or make-up "flair") can be very intimidating to most men. You may be a humble person on the inside, but I can guarantee that is not how you are being reflected on the outside. If you find that you're not getting approached (and your make-up is generally on the very heavy side), try toning it down a bit and see what happens. There are exceptions to this rule, however. Some men, especially ones in the entertainment business are used to this look, and actually prefer it. If you are looking for a music producer, rapper, or perhaps tattoo artist (or the likes), and this is working for you, then by all means, march on.

- **Old sneakers ~** ...or super old shoes in general, really. Now, I'm not talking about your neon Asics that are worn out from running hundreds of miles in them. I do believe that a man can see the value in the fact that you've worked your athletic shoes so hard, and how fit you must be as a result. When I say old sneakers, I am specifically referring to those old white (or black) therapeutic looking sneakers that you wear only for comfort. I understand if you are a nurse and need to wear them to work to be comfortable on your feet all day, but don't you DARE wear them on any kind of date, or even to a place where your future husband MIGHT be (again, barring working in a hospital). Another thing to think about is what's under those shoes. If a man sees that you are okay with wearing your mom's old snow boots from 1987 to church, then what do you think he's imagining your FEET look like? You could have perfectly pedicured feet, but he's most assuredly imagining the worst, which brings us to our next no-no.

- **Bad hygiene and grooming** ~ I really wondered if I even needed to add this one to the list, but it is important, and more than not having bad hygiene, it is important TO have GOOD hygiene. Clean your fingernails, brush your teeth (and gums), wash your hair and at LEAST brush it, don't walk around with food stains on your clothes, and for the sake of EVERYONE, male and female, PLEASE don't smell like body odor! Enough said.

- **A frown** ~ This can be as bad as two layers too many of make-up. A woman with a smile is FAR easier to approach than one with a frown (frowns can be very intimidating). To a man, it can also be a sign of something deeper, such as a toxic or bad attitude. If I only see you with a frown, I am going to guess that you are NOT a pleasure to be around. Now, why would a man desire to ask for any more time with someone like that? Some people have a happy or kind heart, but just don't smile much. If that's you (and even if you are sad on the inside), practice smiling more. Yes, fake smiles: While you're working at your desk, while you're walking down the hall, at the dinner table, and even while sitting on your couch watching TV. Before long, smiling will become a habit and you will be more approachable and inviting to everyone you meet! Be careful not to look crazy or attract creeps, however. There is a "too far" when it comes to smiling at people. Be mindful of where to draw the line.

Some of these truths might have been hard to swallow, or even to believe for some of you, but I challenge you to take this list to a man that you consider worthwhile and ask him if I know what I'm talking about. Some of these items are forgivable, yes, but they are NEVER attractive.

BE GENUINELY BEAUTIFUL

In the end, who you are on the outside - what you act like, what you look like, and the overall "vibe" that you put off – should be a genuine reflection of who you are on the inside. The hope is that, especially after reading this book, you reflect a woman of God who is whole, healed, loving, forgiving, and open-minded; someone who cares about others enough that they want to help when another is in trouble, comfort when another is sad, and pray for someone who is in need of prayer.

The goal is not to fake any of these qualities, but to BE this person on the inside. Where you are lacking, ask God to fill. He will. He loves you, and He wants you AND your husband to be happy and at peace. Ask God to make you peaceful, ask Him

> *A woman with a smile is far easier to approach than one with a frown.*

to help you forgive and heal, and ask Him to help you see the needs of others. Then ask Him to equip you to meet their needs, through His grace. The first step to being an amazing wife is to reflect the love of Jesus from the inside out. Be a genuinely awesome person. This is who you were created to be, and only our Lord and savior, Jesus Christ, can help you to achieve your full potential.

We want our lives NOW to reflect what we will be like as a wife. Let the people around you, including the men, see the wonderful person that you truly are, then some years down the road, continue to be that person. What I'm trying to communicate here is this: don't fake "awesome" to get a man and then turn into someone else. After you marry, be the glorious wife that he imagined you would be. Be a blessing and a refreshment to his soul. Make him thankful to God that He gave YOU to him.

My husband often says that when he looks at me, he knows God loves him. I encourage you: Be the wife that is such a blessing to her husband, that she demonstrates the depth of the Father's love for him. Be genuinely beautiful, from the inside out, so you can not only *win him*, but you will always...

keep him happy.

NOTES

Chapter 4: *Don't Be Eve*

1.   "All the Women of the Bible - Jezebel No. 1." *Biblegateway.com*. Zondervan, 1988. Web. 16 Feb. 2016.

Chapter 5: *Letting Him Off the Hook*

1.   Chapman, Gary D. *Five Languages of Apology: How to Experience Healing in All Your Relationships*. S.l.: Macmillan Reference Usa, 2007. Print.

Chapter 6: *A Man's Three Basic Needs: Men Are Simple*

1. "Why Men Love Women Who Cook." *Elev8 RSS*. Elev8, 29 Nov. 2011. Web. 21 Apr. 2016.

The 5 Love Languages: The Secret to Love That Lasts
- Gary D. Chapman

Personality Plus for Couples: Understanding Yourself and the One You Love
- Florence Littauer

The Power to Forgive
- Reinhard Hirtler

Men Are Like Waffles — Women Are Like Spaghetti
- Bill and Pam Farrel

Love and Respect
- Emerson Eggerichs

Homemakers: A Domestic Handbook for the Digital Generation
- Brit Morin

Why Didn't THEY Tell Me?!: 5 Truths Everyone Should Know About Love
- Love McPherson

Why Singles Are Still Single: 7 Ways Women Block Their Man
- Love McPherson

Made in the USA
Middletown, DE
20 May 2017